Selling

with ☑

Certainty

Selling
with ☑
Certainty

*Straightforward Advice
for Cashing In on the
Full Value of Your Business*

TERRY H. MONROE

GREENLEAF
BOOK GROUP PRESS

Published by Greenleaf Book Group Press
Austin, Texas
www.gbgpress.com

Distributed by Greenleaf Book Group

For ordering information or special discounts for bulk purchases, please contact Greenleaf Book Group at PO Box 91869, Austin, TX 78709, 512.891.6100.

Design and composition by Greenleaf Book Group
Cover design by Greenleaf Book Group
For permission to reproduce copyrighted material, grateful acknowledgment is
made to the following sources:
From "The Facts of Family Business" from Forbes magazine, Forbes.com, July 31, 2013, Copyright © 2013 by Forbes. All rights reserved. Used by permission and protected by the Copyright Laws of the United States. The printing, copying, redistribution, or retransmission of this Content without express written permission is prohibited.
Illustration with caption "OK, Dan, so maybe I should have accepted that final offer." Copyright © by Michael H. Marks. Reproduced by permission of the artist.

Publisher's Cataloging-in-Publication data is available.

Print ISBN: 978-1-62634-536-2

eBook ISBN: 978-1-62634-537-9

Originally published as Cashing In on the Hidden Wealth of Your Business (9781532345210).

Part of the Tree Neutral® program, which offsets the number of trees consumed in the production and printing of this book by taking proactive steps, such as planting trees in direct proportion to the number of trees used: www.treeneutral.com

TreeNeutral

Printed in the United States of America on acid-free paper

18 19 20 21 22 23   10 9 8 7 6 5 4 3 2 1

First Edition

Also by Terry H. Monroe

The Art of Buying and Selling a Convenience Store

The Art of Business Brokerage

TO ALL THE ENTREPRENEURS who have spent hours of hard work building their business, hiring employees, and supporting their families. I hope they will be able to reap the rewards for everything they have invested and toiled to achieve.

Contents

Introduction

"OK, Dan, so maybe I should have accepted
that final offer!"

IF YOU HAVE picked up this book, I commend you. I say this
not because I want to sell more books but because it means
you realize the importance of getting things right before selling your business. I am shocked by how many successful
entrepreneurs—smart folks who've devoted years to building
their businesses—can be so casual and sometimes downright
dumb when it comes time to sell their businesses.

Many of these successful business owners don't take the time to educate themselves on what it takes to successfully sell a business. Instead, they treat it as if they were selling a piece of property or a vehicle—or, worse yet, as if they were holding a yard sale. After years of being in business, often buying and selling items for their company, sometimes they assume that selling the business itself won't be any different. This mindset almost always leaves those entrepreneurs disappointed, frustrated, and with a lot less money in their pocket than they expected.

I've seen this disappointment firsthand in my work as a business broker, having been involved in the sale of more than 500 businesses, and as a business owner owning 40 different businesses myself. And I've learned from my own mistakes, some of which have cost me millions of dollars over the years.

What You Should Know before Selling

Knowing what to do before you sell your business is absolutely critical. Getting the business ready to sell, including making sure you have everything in place, is the most important part of the sale—except for receiving the money for the transaction.

MARKET VALUATION

There are many items that need to be completed before a business can be sold, starting with a market valuation. How can you sell anything if you don't know what it's worth? The answer is you can't; yet so many business owners proceed blindly with selling their business thinking they know what their business is worth, only to later realize they undervalued it and left an excessive amount of money on the table.

TAXES

What about your unseen partner, which so many people seem to forget about? I am talking about the "Taxman" and contending with his wide array of taxes. Chances are you will have to pay taxes on the sale of your business that you didn't even know existed. Remember, taxes are incurred when there is a transaction, and selling your business creates a transaction. So you must make sure you have investigated your tax situation before you decide to sell your business.

More than once I have been in a situation where a business owner wanted to sell their business, only to have them change their mind after they talked with their tax accountant. Why? Because they realized that after paying all the appropriate taxes after the sale, they wouldn't have enough money to live on. Instead, they were going to have to keep operating their business.

PERSONNEL AND BOOKKEEPING

If the taxes work out and you decide you can afford to sell, how do you handle your current business personnel? Having the right personnel will make a difference in what kind of value you can expect to receive. And it might determine whether you can exit at the time of the sale or if you'll need to stay around to facilitate the sale of the business.

Profit and loss statements and well-kept books and records are extremely important for the successful sale of a business. Are your books and records in the proper order and prepared correctly to be shared with a buyer? Will they show the business in the most positive light, or are they in need of being corrected and reformatted? I was once helping sell a business in the $70 million range, and it took me more than a year just to get the company's books and records in order. The owners of the business told me after the first year I worked for them that while they still wanted to sell the business, they were not in a big hurry anymore. By helping them clean up their books, I'd also helped them improve their business.

I had another situation where a business owner wanted to sell but held off because they'd just installed new computer software and said they wanted to wait before selling the business. The new software, however, caused problems and ended up messing up the company's books and records. The business owner waited too long to correct the issues with the software and ended up selling the business a few years later for $4 million less than what it had been worth when we first talked.

THE STATE OF YOUR INDUSTRY

Another thing to consider: What is the state of your industry? Is your business like a video store in the world of Netflix or a bookstore in the world of Amazon? Where your business is situated within its industry makes a big difference. Buyers are generally shopping for businesses that have a long time horizon, and they generally shy away from a business in a declining industry. Business owners who can see changes coming but refuse to differentiate themselves within their industry by initiating changes in their business will be left behind.

A good example of this came when Wal-Mart Stores, Inc., began opening stores around the country, which put a lot of mom-and-pop stores out of business. For a while, there was a cottage industry of consultants who traveled the country, wrote books, and gave talks on how your business could survive when Walmart came to town. Many consultants suggested that owners determine what part of their business was profitable and expand on that area—and of course provide the customer with excellent customer service and knowledge about relevant categories. One of the industries that survived and continued to grow was hardware stores, because they often carried a deeper line of certain categories than the local Walmart did, and they made sure their employees were well versed on the use and implementation of the products they sold. In other words, they differentiated themselves from Walmart and were able not only to survive their new competitor but also to grow.

SALES TRENDS IN YOUR INDUSTRY AND BUSINESS

How has your business been trending over the past three years? As we all know, nothing stays the same in life. Either we are going forward or we're going backward. The sales trends of your business will be a good indication as to what a buyer is willing to pay for your business. Buyers like to buy businesses that are trending upward, because this gives them the indication that the present business owner has been nurturing the business. However, there are times when things happen to a business or an industry over which the business owner has no control. This can limit options for selling and cause the business to show a downward trend for a year or two. Maybe a competitor came into the market. Maybe the business had a very large capital expense that was a one-time cost, such as having to purchase equipment for a special job. Or perhaps there was construction in the area that disrupted the business for a time. Regardless of what the reason is, more often than not, the buyer will notice the downward-trend years and want to know what happened. Unfortunately, even with explanations, some events will tend to hurt the sale of the business.

If I encounter a business that has had two or more years of a downward trend, I will usually tell the business owner to hold off and not sell the business until it has at least stabilized or has started to trend upward. Why? Because selling a business during a downward trend sends a signal to the buyer that the business is in trouble, which usually causes the buyer to walk away or end up making a lowball offer to offset the risk of taking on a struggling business.

FAMILY MATTERS

What is the situation with family members? Do you have another generation to take over? If so, you are probably in better shape than most business owners—as long as you have taken the time to ensure that the next generation is well versed on the operation of the business and not just book smart (lacking hands-on experience).

Are you at the end of the line, without a succession plan? If this is the case, you definitely should continue to read. Or do you have a family member who is part of the business and wants to get out? This can be a big issue and is much more common than you'd think. Especially when there are multiple siblings who all get equal amounts of money from the business but who are not all actively involved in running the business.

PURE PLAY VERSUS GARAGE SYNDROME

Is the business you are selling a pure-play business, or does it have multiple parts that may need to be sold separately? If there are multiple parts to the business, are those parts worth more than the whole?

Can the business be relocated? In today's world, people are more transient than ever. Many buyers want to be able to relocate the business to another area of the country, or perhaps to another country altogether.

I once had an owner contact me about selling his business, which I believed to be a chain of convenience stores and a fuel terminal. Later I realized he owned not only the retail stores and the fuel terminal but also a Dairy Queen and an auto parts store—all wrapped up in the same corporation. I had to take things apart and begin selling the business in pieces instead of as a pure-play business. This is what I call the "garage syndrome"—where the owner of the business started out with one business and, as time went on, kept adding more businesses, doing these acquisitions through the main corporation. In the end, it is like putting everything in your garage and then going in and sorting through everything the business owner has accumulated.

REASONS FOR SELLING

Why are you selling the business? Has there been a change in your life or in your family? Has someone died, gotten divorced, or become ill? What are you going to do after you sell the business? Sounds like a simple question, but in reality, it often determines whether the business will be sold or not. If the business owner does not have some kind of plan as to what they are going to do after the sale of the business, there is a good chance they won't be committed to the process of selling. They might be going through the motions of selling but just fooling themselves. Is there going to be enough money left over for you to survive after the sale of your business?

☑

NOW, MY PURPOSE in writing this book is not to promote my services as a professional intermediary selling privately owned businesses. No, my intention is to help educate and equip business owners so they don't get blindsided and end up not getting the full value from their years of hard work for themselves and their families. And I'm also here to stress to business owners the importance of beginning early as they prepare themselves and their business and not just jumping into selling their business as if they were selling a car or a house. There is a huge difference between the two, and this book will explain those differences and prepare you for what's ahead in selling your business.

I am reminded of an incident where a business owner rushed into the idea of selling his businesses but ended up leaving millions of dollars on the table. A client called me to ask what a certain business might be worth, a business he was looking at buying. I asked him several questions about the possible acquisition and gave him a range value. He told me the seller of the business had just offered it to him for $4 million *less* than what I had estimated was its market value. Why the low price? Because the seller had not conferred with anyone to get a fair valuation. Instead, the seller sought out a buyer—my client—simply because he owned a similar business in the same industry.

Or perhaps the seller was feeling lazy and wanted to take the easy way out.

So please, get the facts and the information available to you as a business owner *before* you set out to sell your business. And be sure you feel comfortable about what you are doing.

I hope this book will get you started in the right direction and help you understand what will be needed from you and other parties to make the sale of your business successful and profitable.

CHAPTER 1

Business Owner: Know Thyself

THE FIRST ITEM we need to address in the selling process is YOU. Believe it or not, this is probably the most important factor in the entire equation of selling. Sellers must be up front and honest with themselves, place their egos aside, and decide for sure if they want to sell. Sellers cannot be, as they say, "half pregnant."

Are You Sure You Want to Sell?

I always start by asking clients: Do you really want to sell? You can't have the attitude that "Oh, sure, I will sell if someone comes along and gives me my price." If you have a half-pregnant attitude, you will have a half-finished sale. In other words, it will never get done. You will flounder and just aggravate yourself and everyone who encounters you.

Let me elaborate a little more about dealing with you, the seller. Making the decision to sell your business is a big deal and can be an extremely hard decision to make. Look at the stuff you have in your garage or storage shed or closets. You haven't sold or gotten rid of all that stuff either, have you? I am using the extra stuff we all accumulate as an example to show how hard it is for us to part with things. When it comes to selling your business, this parting is much, much more difficult.

I got an email from the owner of 11 convenience stores saying she was thinking about selling her stores and getting out of the business. I like getting these kinds of emails, so I immediately called her. We hit it off on a personal level, and she shared with me what she was selling and why she was selling it. She was in her late 50s and had owned and operated the business for over 25 years; she felt the market was right to sell and said—as many would-be sellers do—that she was tired. "Worn out" would be a better way of saying it. The employees and the change in the labor laws and the insurance system had taken their toll to the point, she said, that it just wasn't fun anymore.

I told her I understood. Since selling your business is a hard decision to make, I thanked her for calling me. Then I asked her if she was sure she really wanted to sell or if perhaps contacting me was just a reactionary move on her part. She assured me it wasn't and that she'd been thinking about selling the business for the past two years. "I have received your newsletter and gotten some marketing emails from you," she told me. "And twice I picked up the phone to call you, but I stopped myself." Now, she said, the pain of continuing to run the business was too much. "I decided that I needed more information about selling my business, so I knew I had to reach out to you to get more information."

So we met, and I explained the process to her and estimated what I thought her business would be worth in the marketplace—and how long I thought the process of selling it would take.

Remember, she had been thinking about selling her business for two years before she even contacted me to get additional information. Luckily for her, she was able to sell at the top of the market and get out with top dollar for her business; in another 12 months, she would have missed the top of the market.

Another gentleman I had helped for over 10 years was a CPA by training and a very smart individual; he shared with me that he knew he needed to sell his business and get out. But he couldn't bring himself to pull the trigger, even after he'd done the financial analysis and knew the tax ramifications and the cycle of the marketplace. He ended up selling on the down side of the market because he waited too long.

I am going out on a limb (and will probably get reprimanded for this next statement), but in my experience, it is true: Men have a tendency to wait too long to sell their businesses! They tend to ride the horse too long, as they say, until the horse is about dead—and *then* they make the decision to sell. Women, on the other hand, tend to be more thoughtful and have better intuition as to when it's time to sell. I don't have any scientific data to back up this statement, other than my own experience. But, as you are reading this, think about your situation, and ask yourself whether you are a calculating person who makes decisions based on facts or whether you make decisions based on emotion. I will help you out and give you the answer: We make decisions based on emotion, and *then* we justify them with facts.

So, as you read this book, think about yourself and the way you approach things. If you are thinking about selling your business, consider getting the information now so that when the time does come to sell, you are ready to go—both mentally and structurally. Don't be like my CPA friend who, after I sold his business and we were having dinner, said to me, "Damn, I should have sold two years ago!"

Why Do You Want to Sell?

Just as you need to know yourself, you need to understand exactly WHY you would want to sell your business. Unless you are an individual who falls into the category of sellers who must sell for health, personal, or family reasons, chances are you have a motive and reason to *want* to sell, and you're not in a situation where you *have* to sell. All too often a business owner will put their business up for sale, only to find out after they've started the process that they're not actually ready to sell; they simply *thought* they wanted to sell.

To ensure that you don't fall into this trap, ask yourself this question: What will I be doing after I sell my business?

Are you planning to retire and spend more time with your family? Do you see yourself playing golf, traveling around the world, or enjoying your favorite hobby? Maybe you have another business venture that you want to spend time with? It could be a multitude of things. However, and here is the big however, these are all activities in the future. Unless you have already spent considerable time doing these activities, you are just dreaming and visualizing what you want to do.

Take a Trial Run First

Let me suggest something that may save you a lot of money and possibly grief. If your plans are to sell your business and engage in some of the pleasurable activities listed previously, then I suggest that prior to doing so you take a month off and do just that. Engage in one of the activities that you think you want to do in the years to come. This is like getting a chance to peek into the window—into the future—at what you think you want and get a taste for it before you really do it.

MYTH VERSUS REALITY IN RETIREMENT

For several years I sold businesses in Southwest Florida, selling to people who had moved from the north expecting to spend their days fishing and playing golf and boating. Most of the people to whom I sold businesses had discovered that after selling their businesses up north and moving to Florida and then engaging in their favorite pastimes and hobbies, their new lives weren't what they were cracked up to be. In other words, these folks were bored. If they were married, their spouses were threatening to throw them out of the house if they didn't go get a job or buy a business.

And so that's what most of them did. They bought themselves a job. These former business owners were very capable individuals, and they shared a lot of information with me. One common complaint was that they were disillusioned about what they thought their new lives would be after they sold their former businesses and moved to Florida to settle down and enjoy the good life.

They had failed to distinguish the difference between the end result and the pursuit. Most people enjoy the pursuit more than they do the result. It happens every day. In America, we generally *want* something more than we need it; so therefore, we spend an exorbitant amount of time pursuing the thing we want, only to find out after we have acquired it that we really don't want it as much as we thought we did.

TAKE FOUR WEEKS OFF

Therefore, based on the theory that the pursuit is more satisfying than the acquisition, I have always suggested that prior to engaging in the pursuit, a person should do a trial run. In the case of selling a business, I suggest that a person spend at least four weeks doing the things they think they will be doing after they sell their business to ensure that they really are on the right track—that is, doing what they want to do.

You will discover one of two things. Either you'll find you're unsure about whether the time is right for you to sell your business or you'll feel the time is right and you can't wait to get rid of it. Either way, it will set the stage for the next step, which you cannot proceed to unless you're first mentally prepared.

So, for the first 30 days of the selling process, I want it to be about *you*. In the first week, I want you to take one complete day without being involved in the business. You won't make any calls to people involved with your business, nor will you take any calls from anyone involved with your business. Start out with one day a week, and then work your way up to two days in the first month to get a feel of what it would be like if you were not involved in the business as much as you are now. This is your "trial run" at being away from the familiarity and routine of your business.

RENT AND LIVE LIKE A LOCAL

Remember, when you sell your business, it will be a life-changing experience. I want you to have a preview of what you will be doing later. If after selling your business you will be living in a different geographic area, then I suggest you immediately start spending more time there. Make sure you either rent or buy a place in this new area to get a sense of permanence, living like a local, and that you not approach this new locale with a vacation mindset.

In other words, you need to walk the walk and talk the talk of what you think you want your new life to be. Remember, this will be a new chapter in your life, and you have the opportunity to give this new life a test drive. So go for it—and see how it feels!

CHAPTER 2

Why Business Owners DO Sell Their Businesses

THERE ARE MANY reasons why owners come to the decision to sell their businesses, and these are the most common ones:

- Burnout
- No succession plan
- Expansion
- Profitability
- You can't stop fidgeting with the business
- You outgrow the business
- Dramatic changes in the industry

- Too-rapid growth
- Undercapitalization
- Significant life-impacting events
- The business outgrows you
- Rode the horse too long
- Not focusing on core business
- Favorable tax climate
- Burdensome industry and government regulations
- Limited growth opportunities with limited up side

Burnout

The first and most common reason why business owners decide to sell is burnout. I learned this when I first began selling businesses. I had business owners sit and look me in the eye and tell me how much money they were making but that it didn't matter anymore, because they were tired and burned out. All they wanted was for me to get them out of the business, to help them reduce the stress and drama of running a business full-time so they could move on to another chapter in their life. Having been a business owner and operator of more than 200 retail locations, I could relate to what they were talking about, so I worked to coach them through the process of letting go and learning to enjoy their life after selling their business.

Chances are if you do not have family in the business

with you, especially if you are running the business by your-self without any family or spouse to help you out, then being burned out will propel you to sell your business. Most people do not realize how hard it is to own and operate a business. It doesn't matter what kind of business it is either. Whether it is a dog grooming business or a large manufacturing business, the mental pressures are the same. If you are not physically at the business working, then chances are you are thinking about the business. This goes on 24 hours a day, and it wears on an individual.

Burnout is not uncommon. So, if you're worried that you're some kind of wimp for thinking you can't take it anymore and you are feeling tired and burned out, you are not abnormal at all. You can take vacations and spend more time with friends and family and try to lighten the load, but more than likely the business will take its toll, and you will feel burned out. So don't think you are weak or a failure for having these feel-ings. You are not alone: Burnout is the number-one reason business owners sell their businesses. Sometimes they do it to save their health.

One aspect of burnout is what I call "the thrill is gone" syn-drome. This is similar to the dread factor. You are very capable and know what you are doing, but even the days when your company is profitable no longer get you excited or give you a burst of joy. And when the negative things occur, such as the breakage of items in your business—or, worse yet, receiving notice of an upcoming audit from a state or federal agency—you get upset and overreact, rather than responding with the knowledge that it's all part of running the business.

The old saying is true: You want to make your vocation your vacation—make your work your play—and that way you never have to go to work. If you are feeling the burnout part of your business, take a week or two off, get away from it, and see whether your batteries are recharged when you return. If you feel reenergized, then you are probably OK. But if you still feel burned out, then you may be in "checkout" mode.

No Succession Plan

The lack of a clear successor is another reason why business owners decide to sell. Either the children are not capable of running the business or they're not interested in running the business going forward. Many times the business was the father's dream, and he and his wife have been very successful in building and growing the business. But it doesn't mean the same to the children, because it was not their dream. The business was always there when they were growing up, and they tend to take the business and all the hard work it took to build it for granted.

Not having a qualified successor is more common than you would think. The wise business owner will recognize this and begin the process to sell the business while they are still in control and can direct the destiny of the funds from the sale.

With succession, you want to start early and often. Talk to the person you think will be the successor of the business, and get them started early and actively involved.

A recent client said that his dad started him and his brother in the business when they were in high school, first having them work in various areas of the business and then getting them involved in making decisions. My client said he was upset with his dad for making him do a lot of crummy jobs and putting so much responsibility on him and his brother. But as he got older and the two brothers continued to work in the business and eventually grew it to a large, successful operation, he said they never would have been able to operate the multiple businesses they now own if they had not started at such a young age.

Also, people and situations change. Parents often wait to have the conversation about taking over the business until after their children mature and go to college. But often after the children attend college, they change, and the family business doesn't appeal to them anymore. Which is OK, but children sometimes forget to share this fact with their parents, who are still thinking the kids are interested in working in the family business.

It can be painful to realize that your children don't want to work in the family business. Of course, there is nothing wrong with explaining the opportunities that the family business offers. But forcing the company on your children will only result in resentment or poor performance—or both.

Remember: When dealing with succession, the conversation needs to be both open and often with the individuals who will be part of it. As a friend of mine once told me, "Surprises are for birthdays and Christmas; I don't want any surprises in my business."

WHEN CHILDREN CAN'T BE SUCCESSORS

What if your children are not capable of taking the reins? The reality is that not everyone is capable of running a business, and just because they are your children doesn't automatically make them able to operate and manage your business. Sometimes it takes a lot of courage and mental fortitude on your part to realize this, but it's an important consideration. I have met many clients whose children, despite their parents' hopes and dreams, were not cut out to run the family business.

This is where the saying "Thunder, Blunder, Under" came from. It is when unqualified children are either forced into or allowed into the family business, despite being unqualified to operate the business. By the way, Thunder, Blunder, Under means the first generation made the business successful. The second generation floundered around and somehow kept the business together. And the third generation made or let the business go under.

If nothing else, one thing I have learned from life is that you cannot force a situation, and if you do attempt to force something, it generally doesn't work out for the best.

CHOOSING A SUCCESSOR

Nobody said operating a business was going to be easy, and it can be even harder when you are dealing with family members. I have heard too many stories where there had not been an open discussion about which family member(s) would take the lead role of overseeing the business—especially when it's not going to be the oldest child, who is often the chosen successor. The firstborn isn't always the best choice; some-times child number two or three is more capable and inter-ested in carrying on the business. Be sure to make your wishes clear about your preference for succession, or you could end up tearing apart the family.

One of the best examples I can recall of the first genera-tion making the right decision was in a family business with a second generation consisting of two brothers and a sister. In this situation, the oldest brother didn't care for business operations but enjoyed—and was good at—numbers. So he became the financial controller for the family business, while his younger brother, who enjoyed working with people and had the attitude of an operator, took over operations. The sis-ter oversaw the human resources side of the business.

But the neatest thing about this arrangement was that the first generation had instilled in the three children a strong sense of respect for each other so that no major decision was ever made without all three of them talking about it. Of course they had their disagreements, but their parents rec-ognized the strengths and weaknesses of each of their chil-dren and guided each one of them into the business area that used their strengths. When I arrived, the three owners were in their late 50s and early 60s, and they had been operating the business successfully for 30-plus years.

While it can be difficult to decide on successors and other family matters, it's important that you have these discussions— preferably early and often. You need to know in your heart of hearts whether your children have the ability and fortitude to manage and operate the family business.

Don't do like some business owners and sell the business to your children and then finance it, only to have the children run the business into the ground—causing you to lose the cash flow you were planning on for your retirement, or possibly losing everything. The business will be gone because of weak family members operating it, and your cash flow will disappear too.

FAMILY MEMBERS DISLIKE WORKING TOGETHER

Here, the fact is that although all your kids are capable, maybe they don't get along with each other. If they are not getting along now, it will only be worse once they are in business together. Turning the business over to them will impact your retirement plans, affect their lives, and possibly destroy the relationships they have with each other, which will definitely spill over onto the parents. And if this happens, you can forget the big family gatherings at Thanksgiving and Christmas.

I saw this firsthand recently when I was called in to confer with a family business consisting of eight siblings. A family meeting was called for me to meet and discuss their options with them, but only three of the eight showed up for the meeting. Even though all the siblings worked daily in the family business, there was resentment and unrest among them. They harbored ill feelings toward each other, creating dysfunction within the business. It was only a matter of time before things would begin to unravel and possibly implode.

Worse yet, I had a family—father, mother, their two daughters, and their husbands—who all worked in the business together. Oh, and I forgot the dog that wandered around the office and sat in on meetings too. This was a fourth-generation business. The mom and dad were in their 60s and weren't really working very hard in the business anymore, leaving the bulk of the work to the daughters and their sons-in-law. Things worked great for several years until daughter number two decided she didn't want to be married to her husband anymore and wanted a divorce. This was after she had asked him to move out of their home and she had gotten a new boyfriend. To say there was turmoil in the family workplace would be an understatement.

Daughter number one pulled me aside at an industry function and informed me that she and her husband were on their way out of the business. She suggested that I should get over to their office and talk to her mom and dad. Fortunately, I knew the parents well enough to speak frankly with them. They realized things were not going to get any better, so they reluctantly agreed to sell their business. I was able to get them a cash buyer who bought the business, which removed a lot of family stress. I never did ask the parents how their family gatherings at Thanksgiving and Christmas were after the sale, but I am sure they were a lot more relaxed than the year I worked with them.

Expansion

Another quite common reason business owners DO sell is when the business needs to expand. In these cases, the business needs to be expanded to grow, but the business owner either doesn't want to incur additional debt and liability at their stage in life or doesn't have the ability to acquire the additional funds needed to grow the business.

Most of the time it is nothing more than simple math. Meaning, it will take X dollars to grow to be competitive, and the banks are willing to loan you the money. However, after you figure out how much money it will take to grow to the level you want, and how long it will take to repay the money, you may realize you are going to be too old to do anything, unless you are doing this for the next generation. But if you don't have a next generation, then why would you bother going through all the hassle and risk of borrowing the money and building up the business?

SHOULD YOU BORROW TO EXPAND?

For example, say you are in your mid-60s and it will take you seven to ten years to repay the money you borrowed, but only after you have repaid the money will you reap the benefits of what you have invested. Are you really that excited about working for the next seven to ten years *just* to repay money so that the business may be worth more, only to turn around and then sell the business when you are in your early to mid-70s? Instead of risking your money and your health, you may be better off just selling the business now, unless you think there will be a huge difference in the future value of the business. And if you are that good at predicting the future, then you are miles ahead of the rest of the crowd—and you are definitely an anomaly.

Rather than risking your health and/or money, stand back and run the numbers on what the increased value would be if you did decide to expand the business, and then reduce that amount by 50% because of market uncertainty. Then determine what the business is worth today, and compare the two values. You may be surprised to find that today's situation is a better deal for you than gambling money and time in taking a chance on future dollars.

I recently had lunch with a gentleman who was in his early 50s and who had sold his business a couple of years earlier. He was the second-generation owner. I asked him why he sold his business at such a young age, and he shared with me the sale price of the business, the buyer, and the after-tax dollar amount he netted from the sale (even though I didn't ask for these details). Then he explained that even though he hadn't been ready to sell his business, he knew the offer and the timing of everything were just right. He knew the business would never be worth much more than what it was worth at the time he received the offer, so he decided to take it and move forward.

Then I asked him what he was going to do now that he'd sold his business. That was when he explained to me that by selling the business, he was released from all the daily obligations that went with running it. The freedom he had discovered was unreal and unbelievable in a way he had not anticipated. He knew he would have more time to do different things after he sold his business, but he hadn't realized all the new opportunities that would become available to him. He said that almost every day there was a fresh opportunity that presented itself that he would not have ever seen, or that wouldn't have been available, if he'd kept his business. He said it was as if he had been handed a new life. But this time, he had money in the bank and much more knowledge and experience to recognize good opportunities and know what to do when they presented themselves.

He said in the beginning that he had been concerned and apprehensive about selling his business and about what would happen going forward. But he knew in his heart of hearts that he wanted more out of life, and the only way to accomplish that was to let go of the business and move forward. He did not want to be someone who missed a great opportunity to sell his business and then miss out on what life offered him in the future.

It was a refreshing and enlightening conversation. I only wish other business owners would embrace this attitude and not make the mistake of being a "settler"—settling for the status quo rather than taking a great opportunity to sell their business when that opportunity presents itself.

If you are a business owner who is on the fence, not knowing for sure what you are going to do after you sell your business, you may want to read *The Five Secrets You Must Discover Before You Die* by John Izzo. The author interviewed 235 people between the ages of 59 and 105 to discover what it means to live a full and meaningful life. His interviews with the people are enlightening and heartfelt. He discovered that all the people he interviewed had the same regret about their lives. And that regret was the things they did *not* do! They were not fretting over or regretting the things they had done in life, but rather they regretted not doing things they had wanted to do in their life but had always found an excuse for not doing. They were too busy, they had a job to do, they were going to get to it later, and so on. One excuse after another. Because we all think we are too busy doing certain things, we never get around to doing the things we talk about or imagine doing, so we end up missing out on what might have been some of the best moments of our lives.

I highly recommend this book to business owners. In the past, I sent copies of it to my clients to help give them a new perspective on life, and selling a business can be the beginning rather than the end of your journey.

Profitability

The business is worth more now than it has ever been, and the offering price is too high to resist. You receive an offer you can't refuse, so you make the decision to sell. This doesn't happen very often, but when it does, you should know it is a great offer, and you should take it. Markets go up and markets go down, and regardless of the kind of business you are in, you should always know the market value of your business.

Why not sell your business at the top of the market? This was the situation with Anheuser-Busch, which was purchased by Belgian beverage giant InBev in 2008 for $52 billion.[1] The offer was far beyond the realistic value of the company, and

---

1   Michael J. De la Merced, "Anheuser-Busch Agrees to Be Sold to InBev," *New York Times*, July 14, 2008.

the current generation thought they would be foolish to turn it down. Don't try to convince yourself that you are keeping the company for your kids unless they understand the money involved, loudly declare their desire to run the business, and have a credible plan that makes financial sense. Otherwise, take the money being offered. The adage is: "This is where two fools met. One for offering and one for not taking!"

Over the past several years, I have given presentations across the country to audiences, and my message has been the same. Today is a great time to be a buyer, because money has never been, nor will it ever be again, this cheap to borrow. And it has never been a better time to be a seller, because of cheap money in the marketplace and the historically high valuations of businesses.

To prove my points, just look at the stock market. Valuations are at an all-time high due to the fact that investors are having a hard time finding a place to park their money and earn a decent yield on their investment, and many businesses have been consistent profit-making machines with good returns.

The main pushback I hear from business owners who are reluctant to sell their business when market valuations are high is this: Where can I go to get the kinds of returns that I am making from my business, and where would I park the money to get a decent return? And the answer is: You are right. There is no other place you can make the kind of money you are making from your business now, and there is no place where you can park your money and get really great returns like you are making now.

But in life, everything is a trade-off. If you are healthy and happy running your business and dealing with the daily operations of the business, then you should not sell the business. You should just keep doing what you have been doing. However, if you are tired or burned out from the hassle of running your business, then here is the opportunity to get out when the valuations are high; take the money and just park it someplace safe, because you are out of options.

Trade-offs. This is where many people miss the boat, procrastinate, and don't do anything. They miss the high valuation cycle. Sometimes the cycle never comes back, and they lose both ways. They are still operating their business, but now, because they can't get the money they need out of it, they are unhappy.

Don't be one of the "would have, could have, should have" people. If someone is willing to pay you top dollar for your business, take a serious look at what you're being offered.

You Can't Stop Fidgeting with the Business

I've seen this before: business owners who intentionally implement programs or projects for the business that are not tied to its core products or services. They're doing these things just to have something to do. It is like having attention deficit disorder with a business. You will spend time and money on things that do not relate to the business or the profitability of the business. In these situations, it is best to recognize this problem as soon as possible. If the feeling persists, direct your time and talents toward other projects; for example, get involved with local fund-raisers or community projects that will welcome and appreciate your talents and energy. Just don't mess up the business or its profitability.

If you are on the outside of a business, as I am, this is an easy one to recognize, because I was guilty of this for years. If I wasn't fidgeting with my business, thinking of things to do to it, I was investing in other businesses that distracted me from my core business and the goose that laid the golden egg. Instead of working on what was making me successful, I was messing with low-profit sectors of the business or non-core parts of the business that took both time and money from the business. Don't fall into this trap. Stay focused, or you will be selling because you have to, not because you want to.

You Outgrow the Business

Many people get into business intentionally, and some get into business by accident. Some people are very good at running a business, and after a while they discover that the business they're running is satisfying them personally, but they're not getting the income they wanted. They decide they're ready to move on to bigger and better things.

Now that they know the basics of running a small business, they can use their talents to step up to a larger business that produces more income. For these business owners, it is better to sell the smaller company and move up to the next level. This is similar to changing jobs for people who have maxed out their present position and want a position that's more challenging and rewarding.

If you have mastered the business you presently own and think the business has topped out in what it can produce and that it's not scalable in a way that can be expanded, then chances are it should be sold so you can move on to the next business where you can apply your newfound skills and talents.

Dramatic Changes in the Industry

Market and technology changes can alter the business landscape such that it requires massive reinvestment to reposition the company. Customers tend to migrate to new places and things.

I don't think anybody saw the autonomous car coming, and we haven't even begun to see what offshoots of this new technology will bring. Nor do I think anybody saw the Airbnb business model of renting rooms coming, either. Same with online retailing through Amazon and the multitude of other vendors selling products and services on the Internet. Technology in the marketplace is coming at such a rapid pace that it seems every day a new business is being invented that makes another business obsolete.

To keep up with the trends and desires of your customers, you may need to invest large amounts of time and money, which you are not certain will pay off in the future, but you know not doing so will be the kiss of death. The business is at a crossroads. You must decide whether to take on additional debt to grow the company and attempt to take the company to the next level or sell the business and take your hard-earned equity out now rather than risk losing it all.

ONE OF LIFE'S GUARANTEES—CHANGE

I am a true believer in the law of change, which says that nothing ever stays the same; things are either going forward or going backward. They are either growing or dying.

All industries change, just like people do. But as an industry begins to mature and more players enter, the profitability and future begin to change. For example, would you want to own a video store in today's market? You would probably say heck no, because they're a dying business. And you would be correct.

However, I was in the video rental business before Blockbuster, Netflix, Redbox, and all the other sources of entertainment rental available to us today. And when I began in the business, it was very profitable. But then it began to change. First with the opening of Blockbuster Video stores, then Hollywood Video, and then—well, you get the picture. The point is that the industry changed, just as they all do, until the profitability became almost nonexistent or minimal at best. The key to this change factor is not to stay in your particular industry too long and ride the business into the ground. Be alert. Recognize the changes that are going on in your industry, and be sure to get out before you're forced out of business.

Significant Life-Impacting Events

Nobody likes to talk about significant life-impacting events, but they do occur, and they generally happen to all of us— usually without our having a choice. What is a significant life-impacting event? It could be any number of things: a divorce; a death in the family; an illness, possibly of yourself or of a loved one. It could be the dissolving of a partnership, excessive debt in the business or personal accounts, or the relocation of a loved one. There are many different types of situations that significantly impact our lives.

But sometimes these events may be telling us something. They may be telling us it is time to move on and close the chapter on the present part of our lives and to try something different.

A recent psychological study was done with individuals who were in negative situations and who had many negative components affecting their lives; for example, gangs, domestic violence, and so on. These individuals were removed from their present environment and placed into a more positive one. The results were dramatic. The study proved that if a person were removed from the influence of the negative environment, they could then be reshaped into a positive individual who could use their talents to lead a productive life.

But here was the flip side of the equation: The study also showed that if that same individual returned to the negative situation for a period of 14 days or more, the individual would regress, and all the improvements that had been made in that person's life would be lost. They would be back to square one. So, when a significant life-impacting situation occurs, stand back, look at the situation with an unbiased view, and see whether it is telling you it's time to move on to another business.

Please keep in mind that I am not a pessimist, but I like to refer to myself as a realist. Hence, as a realist I want to look at all the facts and hopefully be prepared for what may occur in the future.

THE DISMAL D'S

Significant events impact us all. These Dismal D's often cause business owners to make significant changes at work and in their personal lives:

- Death

- Disease

- Divorce

- Disaster

- Distraction

- Debt

- Delusion

- Disinterest

- Declining sales

- Dissention among partners

- Disruptive and aggressive competition in the marketplace

- And my favorite one, Dumb

Significant life-impacting events are an unpleasant fact of life, and you can sort of plan for them, but you can never entirely plan for them. You must be prepared.

One day you wake up and either you or a loved one in your family is ill. You know as well as I do that you would give anything you have, especially money, to cure this disease. You want everyone to be healthy. As I have always said, "If something can be fixed with a check, it is not a problem. I can always get more money, but I can't buy health."

Look at Steve Jobs, the co-founder of Apple; even with his billions of dollars, he couldn't beat his cancer and he died. Same for Sam Walton of Wal-Mart Stores, Inc. He was a billionaire too, but his money couldn't cure his disease, and he died.

The same thing goes for a partnership breaking up or a disruption in the marketplace, like what Uber is doing to the taxi business and the sale of cars. And of course, look at how Airbnb disrupted room rentals. Who saw any of that coming?

And the worst unexpected change of all—a sudden death in the family. Recently I called an associate of mine, and we were discussing people we knew who were business owners and how they were doing. When he brought up one individual's name, I said, "Oh, I don't think he would ever be interested in selling his business. He has a great business and really enjoys what he is doing."

My associate responded by saying, "Terry, didn't you know his wife died last year?" Gulp. No, I didn't.

This prompted me to call that business owner, who confirmed what had happened. He said he was thinking about moving on with his life, in a different direction.

Another time I was traveling around talking to past clients and business owners I had known, just checking in, as I like to do. While talking to one gentleman who owned and ran a large company with his family, I asked him how things were going. He said he was selling the company. He had always tried to stay in shape, but one day while he was working out on the treadmill, he had suffered a heart attack. He said that was enough to make him see it was time to sell and go enjoy the rest of his life.

Again—another significant event that changed the course of a business. It happens all the time, and it will happen to you and me.

Partners and parties: They are much alike in the world of business. Many times when you first get into business, you need a partner or a group of partners to get things started. This is normal and usually a very prudent thing to do, because you get to syndicate the risk. It also builds the business with more talent and more money to help the business in its most crucial stages of the start-up phase. However, there comes a time when the partner, who helped bring you to the party, wants to pick up their hat and coat and leave. That is when things can get very interesting.

All too often when partners start a business, they are friends or acquaintances or, worse yet, relatives. Things are great, and everyone is getting along. But then, over time, the reality sets in that this is a real business, and everyone must contribute something to the business, just as everyone is supposed to contribute something to the party. And of course, not all the partners will see the same things or have the same views on all aspects of the business. This is normal, because we are all wired differently, and we all have unique agendas.

But what happens when it is time to break up the party? If there is not a buy-sell agreement in place, then the party could get ugly, and it could very easily lead to the demise of the business if it is not addressed properly and quickly. So don't be the one who gets left out of the party or, worse yet, gets asked to leave the party—empty-handed and emotionally drained. Be proactive, and accept the fact that the party was fun; you learned a lot. Either take your toys and go home or be willing to give the partners some of the toys and send them on their way home. But be prepared, because eventually the party will be over.

The Business Outgrows You

OK, this is a very humbling one, and most people will miss it, but I see it all the time. An individual creates and starts a business, and he is generally good at sales and working with people. He is in an industry that is taking off. He begins to do very well. He continues to do well over the years, and before he realizes it, the business has outgrown him. He still knows how to operate the business, and he is still good at selling, but he only has the ability and education to operate the business at a level equal to his talents and abilities. Ultimately, he ends up stymieing the true growth of the business.

But this isn't the worst part. The worst part is that the business has gotten more complex than when he started it. He needs more sophisticated financial people and financial systems, but he doesn't know where to find them or who to turn to for help. The business begins the process of self-imploding, because all his team members are generally working with limited capabilities just as he is. Their accountants are ones that he has had for years, and they will continue to do the same things. They can't help the owner grow, because they have the same problems he has. And the same is true for the rest of the employees and advisors. It is like the blind leading the blind.

So the business begins a slow death if it isn't sold or merged with a more sophisticated business to help take it to the next level. Beware, because this one will sneak up on a business owner, and unless they have strong self-esteem, they will not recognize it, and their ego will keep them in denial. The business will be on a downhill slide.

If this happens, stand back, take an assessment of yourself, and try to find someone who can help you recognize that it may be time to sell or merge your business.

I saw this situation play out in front of me several years ago, when a business owner called me to look at the distribution business he had built from scratch. He knew he was doing very well and was at a crossroads with his business, but he didn't know what to do next, so he wanted me to look at his situation. Yes, his business was very profitable. But it was a mess. He had grown so fast that his infrastructure was antiquated, and he was unable to properly track his accounts receivable, which were in the millions. His sales department was in complete disarray, and his back-office management system was still being overseen by the same woman who'd helped him start the business. They were working with bad financial software, and the business was about to implode.

Fortunately, he was open-minded, and I was able to convince him to make a few changes. We then sold the business to a very large company that wanted to be in the industry sector in which my client was operating. The business owner received a large cash amount for his business, and he continued to work for the new company for several years afterward.

Rode the Horse Too Long

I use the term "horse" when I am referring to a business. I have watched business owner after business owner continue to stay in the same business and not make any substantial changes to the business: They just keep doing the same until the business dies a slow death. The sad thing about this is that they know what they are doing, and yet they continue doing it.

Recently I had numerous conversations with a man with whom I have worked for over six years, this time to discuss whether he might be interested in selling his business. Several years ago, I had even done a market valuation to help him determine what his business was worth. The business was profitable and employed quite a few people. It was a second-generation business. Overall, I thought it was a good business and was definitely salable. The owner of the business was in his 60s, about retirement age. The owner and the business had all the signs of a makeable deal if the business were taken to market.

But then something strange happened. The owner of the

business basically fell off the radar. There was very little communication between us, and when we did communicate, it was short and not very detailed. Since my work with business owners sometimes spans years, I didn't get too concerned, because I believe you have to let things flow and never force any type of deal or push someone into a situation for which they are not ready.

Then, after a couple of years with very little communication, I mentioned to a colleague (the person who'd originally introduced me to the business owner) that he might want to contact the business owner and check his status. So my colleague contacted him, only to learn that the fellow was in serious financial straits. It was so bad that the business owner had gotten himself into a negative cash flow position and was in the "workout" department of his bank.

Let me explain the workout department. If you have ever had a business loan with a bank, then you know that with the loan come certain obligations that are required of the borrower for the loan to stay compliant with the bank's policies. These obligations are called covenants, and if you don't adhere to the covenants of the loan, then the bank can call their note due—in other words, ask for their money back immediately.

However, with business loans it isn't always as it sounds. For example, my partner and I once built and operated an Arby's restaurant, and it was taking longer than we had anticipated for the restaurant to provide positive cash flow. After having to inject money into the restaurant for about two to three years, the bank wanted to get rid of our loan, because they felt we were too risky for them.

But they couldn't call the note due, because they realized it was less risky to have us continue to operate the restaurant than to force us to close the restaurant down and sell the property. So they moved our loan from the normal loan department of the bank to the workout department. At this stage, the bank constantly calls you and monitors your loan and your capability to pay it back. If they begin to feel the risk is too great for the bank or that you can't personally fund the loan with outside sources of income, then they have the authority to foreclose on your loan.

Often these "workout" folks are not very nice people. Some of them are so bad they make the IRS look good—and it takes a lot for that to happen! If you have made it to the workout department of your bank, you are generally in trouble. More than likely the bank has already taken the write-down of your loan within the bank (thus reducing the book value of your assets), and they're going to start acting like an unforgiving bill collector. They will work with you for a while, trying to get your loan back into compliance, but if they see there is too much risk involved, they will either strongly encourage you to sell the business or they'll call the note due, which will force you to sell. Either way, it is not a pleasant situation. Not everybody can survive the financial strain—or, worse yet, the mental stress—that goes with being in a bank's workout department. (In the case of our restaurant, we were fortunate that sales increased enough to fulfill our obligations to that bank.)

Well, to continue the story of the gentleman at the start of this section, even though his company was going down, he refused to reach out for guidance or ask for advice from people who could have helped him. He had ridden the horse too long. The horse (his business) was barely able to walk. We were called in at the end of the business cycle. Fortunately, we were able to find a cash buyer who could pay enough for the business that the owner was able to satisfy the bank and still put some profit in his pocket and maintain his ownership of several other small businesses.

The moral of the story: When you are in a hole, quit digging. There are always people who are qualified and who can and will help you if you will just give them the opportunity. I really liked that business owner who got himself in the workout department of the bank, but since I'm not a mind reader, I had no idea he was having financial issues. When I reviewed his books and records, all I saw was that his business was thriving and profitable. He didn't tell me otherwise. Some people will just clam up, not do anything, and just keep digging.

Not Focusing on Core Business

I know this reason for selling probably better than anyone else, and that is because for many years I had a terrible disease. It is a disease that you won't find in the medical books, but it is a real disease, and it can and will cost you lots and lots of money. I know this on a very personal and intimate level.

DEALITIS

The disease I am referring to is called "dealitis." And it consists of the inability to focus on one business; instead, you are constantly chasing another deal to add to your portfolio of businesses that you already own and operate.

With dealitis, I owned and operated between six and seven businesses at one time. I couldn't find a deal I didn't like. I ended up owning multiple restaurants, manufacturing companies, a television station, a radio station, a motel, a convenience store, several real estate companies, a few commercial development companies, and dozens of retail outlets. I even owned a ladies' dress shop.

I had the disease bad. And I found out that if you don't find a cure for this disease, it will wreck your life. You'll be running around like a chicken with your head cut off to keep from becoming financially broken, because you are not able to focus on your core business. And your core business is where the money is and where the money comes from to support your habit of buying all the other businesses that you think you need and, worse yet, think you will be good at operating.

I share this with you so that you will be on the lookout for dealitis and won't fall into the same trap I did, where I kept buying or starting businesses just for the thrill it gave me. Doing this does give you a thrill and an adrenaline rush, but it can be very costly. And I say "costly" because even though you are successful at one business, it doesn't mean you will be successful at others.

Sure, you probably have the intelligence to own and operate a different kind of business, but here is the rub: Every kind of business takes a specific skill set, and there are nuances to each. Therefore, you will basically be paying tuition to learn these different nuances of the new businesses. And tuition can come in many forms—in this case, money and time.

What is the first rule of business? Don't lose money! And the second rule of business? Read rule #1.

And losing time is even worse. We can always get more money, but we can never get more time. How dumb is it to be wasting time on a new business venture that may make us some additional money, when what we should be operating is our core business and the business that brought us to the party? Now, I am not saying you shouldn't consider new investments and extensions of the business you are already in. What I am saying is that all too often someone gets the wild idea that they need to be in such and such, and like a dog chasing a car, they take off in a different direction and end up costing themselves time and money.

The funny thing about dealitis is that the disease was not exclusive to me. I've since discovered that there are other people who have it; they just don't realize they have it. They start to tell me about all the things they are doing and the different businesses they are buying and how they are having some issues with their new ones.

I recently was talking with one of my longtime clients whom I thought I knew pretty well. Come to find out that I didn't know as much about this person as I thought. We were having a conversation about selling off some underperforming assets of his very profitable chain of convenience stores when the subject of a Harley-Davidson dealership came up. Now, I knew that he and his family were into motels, grocery stores, trucking, and the distribution business, but where in the world did a Harley-Davidson dealership come from? I couldn't help myself and asked him to elaborate.

He explained that a couple of years earlier, his family was offered the opportunity to buy half of a Harley-Davidson dealership in a town that was out of their market area. It was being operated by an individual who had never been in the motorcycle business. It wasn't performing very well, but my client thought since he and his family were successful at operating their businesses, they could apply their expertise to the Harley-Davidson dealership and make it profitable. So they purchased half of it.

I'll admit I was dumbstruck. I knew that just because someone is successful at one business doesn't mean they will be successful at other businesses. Especially if the new business is likely to require specialized knowledge, as in this case.

This, I believe, is an illustration of dealitis. Here was a highly successful business owner and family who had thought that because they were successful at their core business, they could add a new and unfamiliar business that would be successful, too. Unfortunately, the motorcycle add-on was a failure.

Now, here is the sad thing about a situation like this—and again, I know this from firsthand experience: When an individual gets caught up in dealitis, it is extremely distracting. It is distracting not only to your core business but to your family, too. Anyone who has ever owned and operated a business knows that you are working 24 hours a day on your business. When you are not physically working at the business, you are thinking about the business. It never stops. We can't help it. It is the way we are wired, and this is what makes the difference between an employee and an entrepreneur.

So sometimes businesses get sold because the business owner, after losing money or time or both, wakes up and decides it doesn't make sense to keep this extra business they thought they should have started or purchased. Instead, they head back to the core business they began with.

I once heard that the secret to success is to find out what is working for you and do more of it—and find out what is not working for you and do less of it. Good advice.

CHAPTER 3

Why Business Owners DON'T Sell Their Businesses

WHILE THERE ARE many reasons why people choose to sell their businesses, there are fewer reasons people choose *not* to sell—and often those negative reasons exert even more influence on a reluctant seller. These negative reasons range from money to ego and encompass a lot in between.

The Rule of 72

Want to double your money? In the world of finance, we do this by using the "rule of 72." To find this, take the interest rate (or rate of return) and multiply it by the number of years it takes to get to 72—and that is how long it will take to double your money. An example would be if you were earning 6% interest on your money, then you would multiply 6% × 12 years = 72. It would take 12 years (at 6%) to double your money.

However, in the world of selling your business, my rule of 72 says that if a business owner is still alive at the age of 72 or older (and this generally applies to men), then the business owner will die with the business—and *not* sell it. Do you know why? Because the business becomes their identity. They can't separate themselves from it. Their ego has taken over; they are known around town and among their friends as the pizza guy or the gas station guy or the computer guy. And because the business is their identity, generally no amount of money will separate them from it.

Many people don't believe me when I say this, until I show them examples.

One time I showed up to a business-sale closing. Everyone was there: the buyer, the banker, the title people, the attorneys. Everyone, that is, but the seller. He'd backed out and never showed up. Of course the deal died. The seller was in his late 70s.

Another time, I had a purchase agreement signed. On the way to the closing, the seller told me he couldn't go through with the deal, admitting it was too hard for him to sell. He wrote me a check for my services and told me to go away. In this case, the seller was in his 80s.

In another case, we not only had the purchase agreement signed; we were through the due diligence period and were scheduled to close. This time the seller couldn't bring himself to sell, even though his entire family was on board with the sale. He canceled the deal and wrote the buyer and my company a very large check just so he wouldn't have to sell the business, and it cost him and his family millions of dollars. He was in his early 70s.

I was talking with a business owner who said to me, "Terry, I am only 58 years old, but I have let the business become my identity, and I don't think I could ever sell it." This was after he told me that his children were not interested in the business, his wife didn't want to have anything to do with the business, and to top things off, his doctor told him he was having some serious health issues that he needed to address. I commended him for sharing the details with me. But I felt he was in serious denial of his situation, he was putting his family in a very precarious place, and his attitude was quite selfish.

Profitability + Ego = Intelligence. Not!

You would think this would be the easiest one to see and to address, but in the scheme of things, this one is probably the most damaging of all. The business is not profitable, hasn't been profitable for a while, and chances are it's never going to be profitable.

I was recently contacted by a business owner who owned about 30 convenience stores, 10 of which were not making money and hadn't made any money for several years. I showed the owner how I could help him get these 10 stores off his books and increase his profitability by 30%. I even offered to go close the stores for him so he wouldn't have to face the employees.

But the owner couldn't bring himself to pull the trigger and make the decision—and to this day this chain of stores is losing hundreds of thousands of dollars a year due to one person's ego. Believe it or not, this is common. These are educated people who, like all of us, have an ego. Yet somehow, they've let their egos cloud the part of their brain that relates profitability and business. Businesses are created to make a profit—period. Yes, sometimes people get into business to buy themselves a job, but overall, business is designed to make a profit. And when it is not making a profit, it is not a business; it is an ordeal.

I find the situation involving ego more prevalent with men than with women. It reminds me of why GPS was invented for cars—because men don't like to ask for directions!

But on the serious side of things, men have more of a problem with ego than women do. For some reason women can look at a situation and apply the facts of reality to it and then do what needs to be done, but men let their egos get involved and move the facts to the back of their minds.

Now, I realize I'm generalizing here, but this is a serious issue and is far more common than you might imagine. I feel it's important to discuss this reality, because if the ego issue is not addressed, it can cause a family much financial and domestic harm.

Recently I had a situation where there were two brothers who owned a business together. They had owned the business for over 20 years, and the younger brother was the lead partner, because the older brother was running another business that the two brothers owned. They decided to sell the business that the younger brother was operating, but what no one realized was that even though both brothers agreed to sell the business, the younger brother deep down could not let go of the business.

He began doing something subversive, which, if you don't watch for, you won't catch. What am I talking about? Well, the younger brother would go through all the motions of providing me with all the information I needed to get the business on the market for sale and to engage with the buyer, but then he would begin to sabotage the transaction. At first, I didn't catch this happening, but after the second transaction fell apart in which we had a buyer under contract, I realized what the younger brother was doing.

You might think this sounds crazy—and it is somewhat crazy—but the younger brother, who was in his late 50s, had gotten himself in a position where he had been operating and managing the business for more than 20 years, and now, in this part of his life, he wasn't sure of himself moving into the older brother's business. The younger brother had a feeling of inferiority. He was subliminally sabotaging the transaction by being combative with the buyer and explosive in his responses about buyer requests for due diligence— reactions that were all unfounded. With any issue that arose, the younger brother blew up. He said he wasn't going to do such and such and that the buyer didn't need the requested information, when in truth he was wrong. The buyer did need the requested information.

And to make matters worse, the attorney who was representing the brothers would not stand up against the younger brother. He capitulated to his demands and incorporated frivolous requests into the purchase agreement rather than standing up to the younger brother and telling him no. And the reason the attorney was a lay down? Because he was getting paid by the hour and didn't really care if the transaction closed or not. The attorney didn't want to lose the work he was getting from the client, and if the business were sold, then there would be less money for him going forward. So he, too, was subliminally sabotaging the transaction by being an accessory to the situation!

I know this sounds extreme, but this is for real and not the first time I have seen this type of behavior, so you must be on the lookout for it—both in a seller and in the attorney or accountant working on the deal.

It was only after we got to the third buyer—and, I might add, for several million dollars less than the first two buyers—that I was able to get the older brother to recognize what was happening and get him involved to take control of the situation. We finally got the business sold. The younger brother and the money from the sale were consolidated with the older brother's business, and the two brothers worked together as owners going forward.

Just because someone tells you they are going to do something and they really want to sell, it may not be the true situation. Having a business owner sabotage their own deal is not as uncommon as you would think. I have more stories about owners sabotaging their own business sales.

Here is an example I will leave you with. Most often the owner of a business is a very intelligent individual who can communicate with customers, vendors, and a multitude of other people. They have made money over the years, and there-fore they think they are smart about other matters outside their own business. But thinking that *being a business owner + profitability + ego = intelligent about more worldly matters outside their business* is a formula for disaster. So the business owner decides they want to sell their business, and instead of hiring a professional intermediary and business transaction attorney and conferring with a good tax accountant, they decide to sell the business themselves, because of the formula:

profitability + ego = intelligent about more worldly matters

You know what generally happens? Nothing. Because the owner isn't really serious about selling—or they would have brought in the proper people to get the job done, and they would have listened to those experts. It is like someone going to the doctor and explaining the symptoms they are expe-riencing, and the doctor telling them what they believe is wrong, and then the patient arguing with the doctor because they did their own research on the Internet and they believe something different is wrong with them.

Bring in a professional. You wouldn't do your own surgery! Sounds bizarre, doesn't it? But this happens more times than you can imagine. If you are a business owner, you must be on the lookout for this type of thinking and not let yourself go there. If you are a party to someone who is in the process of or is going to be selling their business, you need to be on the lookout for this type of behavior, or it may cost you a lot of grief and money.

Are You Too Comfortable in Your Business?

I believe most business owners get too comfortable in their businesses and therefore never decide to consider selling or making changes. They are comfortable in the fact that it is easy to show up to work in the same place every day. They are making enough money to support their present lifestyle. They have gotten some age on them and no longer have the same energy they had in their youth, so in essence, they don't want to work any harder than they do presently. They like the business as it is, and they don't want to implement all the new technology or new systems that would or could improve it. They have lost their desire to grow the business, because they are comfortable, so they choose to ignore the outside elements and keep doing what they've been doing, assuming things will be fine.

Like having too much ego, this attitude is more prevalent among men than it is among women. I am not trying to be sexist here, just recognizing a reality. Men tend to be more willing to settle—I call them "settlers"—than women, and it shows in the way men operate their businesses. And they'll continue to be settlers until there is an issue that arises and forces them to make a change.

I am not going to teach Psychology 101 here, but life is built around the fact that as human beings we do things either for pleasure or to avoid pain. If the situation is not uncomfortable and isn't exerting some kind of pain, then the individual will not make a change; instead, they'll just remain where they are.

To give you an idea, I will share a story about my longest-running client relationship, which lasted for ten years before I finally sold his business. When you first hear this, you might think, *Wow! Terry must not be very good at what he does if it took him ten years to sell one business!*

Well, here is the rest of the story.

My seller was a great guy who acted as though he wanted to sell his business. It was a fairly large business, and after I'd work for many months to sell it and we'd get close to getting a deal put together, my client would back off. He'd go into hiding, coming up with an excuse about why the time wasn't right to sell the business.

This went on for about nine years, until something painful happened. The business was sued by a group of employees and a tenacious attorney who would not back off. The suit was eventually settled, but the business owner got a wake-up call and realized he had stayed in the business too long and knew he should have gotten out sooner. Everything ended well. To this day, the business owner and I still talk about why it took him so long to get out of the business, and he admits he was the issue.

As a wrap-up, while there may seem to be fewer reasons for NOT selling a business than for selling it, these negative forces often exert more pressure on business owners—often with detrimental outcomes.

CHAPTER 4

Are You Prepared to Sell?

LET ME START this chapter by answering the age-old question: WHEN is the best time to sell your business?

Actually, this is easy to answer. The best time to sell your business is when you don't have to.

Many business owners are reluctant to sell in good times because they are making a lot of money, and they won't sell in bad times because they can't get full value.

But the best time to sell any business is when you *want* to.

Remember—every business owner will exit their business sooner or later. It is up to you whether it will be on your terms or someone else's.

I like to say that I am one of the most fortunate people in the world, because I get to work with some of the most successful business owners in the country. Working with and around these successful individuals is not only illuminating, but also invigorating when it comes to the world of business and entrepreneurship. These folks take the daily challenges of operating their businesses in stride, regardless of whether they're dealing with new regulations that are thrown at them or the many vendor and employee issues that abound daily. They are competent in what they do and, more than likely, are underappreciated by their peers and family.

Maybe I have such a deep appreciation of these individuals because I have operated some 40 different businesses. But one fact remains from all my past relationships with these business warriors: When it comes to selling something, they are reluctant to pull the trigger—especially when it comes to selling their businesses.

Buying Is Easy; Selling Is Tough

After many years of working with hundreds of competent business owners, I believe I have finally identified the problem. It's pretty simple. It is easier to buy than it is to sell.

Sounds too simple, doesn't it? Maybe that's because it really *is* simple.

You see, anybody can buy something. You don't have to be smart to buy something; all you need is either the money or the available credit. You can negotiate a better price, but you won't know if you got a good deal until later, either when you operate it and see if it's profitable—or when you sell it. So, even if you overpay, you can still buy something. It really is easy to be a buyer.

But to be a seller is harder. To sell something involves many different emotions. I am guilty of being a bad seller. I don't like to sell my stuff, and I bet that you and most other people are the same way. There is something about our "stuff" that makes parting with it difficult. Sometimes it gets so bad that people rent storage buildings for their stuff, knowing they will never get it out of storage, but they are too weak to sell it or give it away. So, instead, they continue to pay monthly storage fees for years. I know this happens, because I have several friends in the storage business, and they told me about having to open a storage unit after a tenant, who had paid for years on end, quit paying. They found a bunch of old clothes and junk nobody would ever use or want.

To make the decision to sell your business is a big deal. It can make someone an emotional wreck. Just the thought of selling a business can make a person sick to their stomach and cause depression or excessive stress.

I share this with you so that you won't think you are alone in having these feelings. After putting all the facts and figures together, I know it should be easy to determine whether selling the business is the right thing to do, but I didn't say it was the easiest thing to do.

To begin with, you must get yourself into the proper mental mindset before you begin the journey of selling your business.

Lay out all the facts. Ask yourself why you want to sell the business. In chapter 2, I listed many reasons why people sell their businesses, and one of those reasons may fit your situation. After you have looked at the facts and have come to determine that selling your business is what you want to do, you are halfway there. Having the mental stamina to begin and then staying with the process of selling your business is not easy, but it can be very profitable and satisfying once your business is sold.

Of all the businesses I have sold, and they list in the hundreds, I have never had anyone come back to me and say they wished they had *not* sold their business. Quite the opposite happens, actually. I have lots of business owners who come back to me and thank me for helping them get out of business. Their only regret was that they didn't do it sooner.

So be prepared to work hard, but stay the course and don't give up. In the end, you will be happy you followed through and sold your business. Remember, it is easier to buy than it is to sell; you can always be a buyer, but not everyone can be a seller.

Reasons Sellers Procrastinate

Let me share with you a few reasons why many business owners procrastinate when it comes to selling their businesses and why they are not able to stay the course when they begin the selling process.

IT IS A LOT OF WORK

Believe it or not, when it comes time to sell almost anything, especially if it's your business or source of income, it is a lot of work. Before you can sell anything, you have to know what you are selling—meaning you will need all the same information that you would want to know before you were to buy the same business. For example, if you were the buyer of a business, you would want to know—

1. How much is it doing in sales and income? In what direction is the business trending? Up or down? If down, you had better have a good reason or the price will be reduced according to the trend.

2. How long have you owned the business, or when did you start it?

3. What do the profit and loss statements say for the past several years?

4. What do the tax returns look like, and why are they different from the profit and loss statements?

5. What are you really getting when you buy the business? Real estate, equipment, accounts payable, accounts receivable?

6. Are there any liens against the business?

7. What is the situation with the employees? Are there any outstanding employee issues with violations pending?

8. Are there key employees, and if so, are they under an employment agreement?

9. What about intellectual property?

10. Are there special licenses or permits that will need to be acquired or transferred to the new owner, and if so, how long does this normally take to accomplish?

As you can see just from the few items mentioned in this list, it can be a daunting task to assemble all the needed information to sell a business, and without a checklist and a coach, the process just gets more difficult. Later in this book when I share with you what a due diligence list looks like, you will thoroughly understand that it is a lot of work to sell a business. It is nothing like having to sell a car, where the only thing that may be involved is a car title and maybe a bill of sale.

IT IS STRESSFUL

Do you want to know one of the top reasons for high blood pressure? You would be right if you said stress. Yes, stress is at the top of the list as the cause for many different sicknesses. Most of the time, stress can be avoided simply by planning and delegating.

After you've invested a lot of time in negotiating and preparing information, and it's time for the buyer to make an offer, sometimes the deal falls through, and you are back to square one. And sometimes you are further behind than where you started, because of the distraction of the ongoing sale. This makes the selling process very stressful. Most people don't think about factoring stress into the equation of selling—but it is a very real part of the process. With preparation and guidance, however, you can be prepared and thus reduce the amount of stress during the sale.

I had one seller who got so stressed out during the process of negotiating the purchase agreement that he had to take time off to get ahold of his emotions. It is not unusual for a seller to start screaming and threatening me and everybody around them, because the stress has gotten so great for them. Fortunately for me, I can see this coming and am prepared for it. Nobody likes to hear someone yell and become emotional, but having been through the selling process myself, I can empathize with them and understand their situation. We always work through it.

It can become even more stressful when there is more than one seller, for example, when the seller is a partnership or, worse yet, a family business with multiple family members involved. Trying to please many individuals becomes almost impossible if one of them is a reluctant seller or has some animosity for other family members. Having a reluctant seller as a partner will cause both grief and stress.

YOU DON'T KNOW THE PROCESS

Selling a business is really a staged process, which, when done properly, reduces the stress of the situation and steers the buyer and seller to the closing table. However, most people don't sell complicated things like a business very often, so they don't realize there is a process. They end up doing things in a haphazard way that could cause them grief and confusion.

The key is to put together the right team of players— people who have experience selling complicated things like a business. In the sale of a business, the team will need a business intermediary, an accountant, and an attorney—in that order. With the team working together, they will complement each other and work within the process, ultimately getting you top dollar for your business and doing it painlessly.

Selling a business is no different from what an attorney does when he enters the courtroom to try a case. He has a plan, a list of questions, and a process for how he wants to try the case or defend it. The same goes for a doctor. When doctors go into surgery to operate on someone, they don't just show up and think since they've done this before, they'll just wing it and see how things go. No, they have a process for how the procedure should be performed. Likewise for a pilot. Having been a pilot, I know and understand how crucial a checklist is. Regardless of how many hours a pilot has in the left seat of a plane, he will use a checklist before takeoff, during flight, and during landing. There is a process, and you don't want to miss a step.

If your biggest financial asset is your business, don't you want to make sure you hire someone who has plenty of experience in selling a business? Someone who knows the process and shares with you what the process is, so you don't get blindsided, possibly hurt financially, and forced to deal with unwanted stress? Of course you want that, and that is why you hire someone who knows and understands the process of selling a business.

IT CREATES FEAR

Regardless of what an individual is selling, there is always the fear that they are selling too low and thereby leaving too much money on the table. It is essentially the fear of the unknown. So how do you know if you are selling too low? Easy. Do the research before you decide to sell your business and take it to the marketplace.

In today's world, there is hardly anything that is private. People find out things about each other in numerous ways. Finding out what a business like yours is selling for in the marketplace is not going to be very difficult in the Internet age. Plus, you can ask other individuals who may belong to your trade association. Ask them if they know of any recent sales that you can compare with and who helped facilitate the sale. Trade associations can be a good source for business sellers and their sales team members. It may pay to contact the head of the trade association and ask them. Ask a knowledgeable business intermediary if they have sold any businesses like yours and how much they sold for.

All you need to do is ask around in a few certain places, and you will have a price range for what your business should be worth in the marketplace. But in the end, you should confer with a professional who understands your business and your industry, because an experienced professional can provide you with factual data to give you a valuation of what your business is worth in the current climate. Just as you don't want to diagnose a sickness you may think you have by Googling your symptoms, the same applies to selling your business. You can search on the Internet, ask a fellow business owner, and talk to your trade association, but in the end, you will need to talk to a professional who works with business owners in the sale of their business, such as a business broker or an investment banker.

I recently represented one of the smartest business owners I have ever worked with. He was a certified public accountant (CPA) by trade with a high IQ and a low tolerance for people who weren't efficient or didn't do their jobs properly. He had a very successful business, and only after talking to him off and on for two years did he feel comfortable enough to work with me and let me represent him in the sale of his business. He told me that first he wanted to make sure I knew what I was doing. So, for two years, he'd been interviewing me and checking me out. And this was just to get started with him. Even though he questioned me on everything I did and on information I requested from him regarding the business, he shared with me that he knew he was smart enough to sell the business himself.

However, the business represented his retirement money. He knew that if he tried selling the business himself, there would be mistakes. He would be learning and figuring out who to talk to, how to market the business, and the sale process. He didn't have time to learn all this, and the sale of his business was only going to happen one time. He was going to school with me so he could understand everything and know what was going on, but he gave me the latitude I needed to get the business sold. Fear was involved. It was his fear of messing the deal up and thereby impacting his retirement money. Because of this fear, he did the right thing by hiring an intermediary, consulting with his accountant, and hiring a good business transactional attorney.

YOU FOCUS TOO MUCH ON THE PRICE

Generally, the first thing that comes into your mind when getting ready to sell something, especially if it is as important as your livelihood, like a business, is what to price the business at. What is the highest price I can get for it?

Don't get me wrong, but getting the highest price shouldn't be your ultimate goal. No, what you should be focused on is this: How much do I get to put in my pocket when the sale is complete? There is a difference between the selling price and how much you get to keep after the sale is complete.

All too often a seller will come up with a price that a buyer agrees to pay. But it is only then that the seller goes to talk to his accountant and learns a quick lesson in taxes. Oh yes, we forgot about the other partner that you have had all along but neglected to recall in the selling process. That partner, of course, is the Taxman.

The point is, before you decide to sell anything, when you have a general idea of what your business will be selling for, be sure to go talk with your accountant. Have them run the numbers to see how much money will end up in your pocket before you complete the sale. You may be surprised, and not in a good way, to find out you cannot afford to sell. Or perhaps you'll discover there's a better way of selling that will enable you to put more money in your pocket.

Word of caution when talking to your accountant: You may want to get a second opinion. Consider the scenario of going to your doctor, and he tells you that you need surgery. You'd rather not have the surgery, but you don't want to hurt your doctor's feelings by going to another doctor for a second opinion. But reluctantly you do get a second opinion, and you find out you don't need the surgery. So then you no longer feel bad about getting the second opinion, and you are probably a little upset with the original doctor who recommended the surgery.

Well, it's the same with selling your business. Remember, chances are that the largest financial asset you have is your business, and you are only going to get one shot at selling it. You want to make sure you are correct when it comes to how much you will owe in taxes, because the last thing in the world you want is to sell your business and pay the taxes you believe are owed on the sale, only to find out a couple years later (after you sold your income-generating business) that you owe more taxes on the sale of the business, *plus* penalties and interest! And believe me, the IRS has no sense of humor or compassion when it comes to owing them money.

So you may want to get a second opinion on how much you will owe in taxes on the sale of the business before you put the business on the market, because you want to know before the sale how much money you will net from the sale.

You Are Not a Superhero, and You Are Not Going to Live Forever!

Most people do not like change. Instead, they want things to be constant and uneventful, and they delude themselves into thinking that nothing will change—that everything will stay the same and everyone will live happily together forever after.

The truth is that most people will have those significant life-impacting events we discussed in chapter 2: a death in the family, a divorce, someone getting sick with a disease, additional debt that would impact the business and your life, a split in the business partnership . . . the list goes on. It is generally no one's fault. It is just part of the journey of life, and you should be somewhat prepared for it.

So be prepared and have a plan B for unforeseen events that may befall you or your family. Be prepared so you don't get caught and end up with the possibility of losing everything, when, with a little planning, it could have been prevented. Again, use your team. Update the market value of your business that the intermediary shared with you. Use your accountant to make sure all the taxes are paid and there will not be any unknown taxes outstanding. Work with your attorney to have a plan of succession in place to keep the cash flowing in case you aren't around.

Without fail, I will get a call from a seller who is frantic, because either they had some kind of medical issue, or something changed in the business—such as a competitor coming into the market. Even though they knew about it, they waited too long, clinging to the hope that something would change and the issue would disappear or go away. But it never does. It only gets worse, and by delaying and procrastinating, these business owners generally cost themselves and their family a considerable amount of lost money and grief that could have been avoided.

It is better to adhere to the actions of the Boy Scouts and their motto, "Be prepared," than to get caught unprepared.

Rely on Professionals

This old saying is right on the money: He who represents himself has a fool for a client. How does this relate to selling your business? Because everybody at one time or another has sold something, and some people have sold many things. Therefore, they think they are an accomplished salesperson. Surprise! Guess what? You may have hurt yourself more than you know.

Imagine you are in court and you are representing yourself, and on the opposing side is a team of professional lawyers who practice law every day and have done so for 20 years. Do you think they may have an advantage over you when it comes to knowing the process, the players, and the system? Of course they do. Righteousness will only take you so far. Who wants to take such a chance when you are dealing with your livelihood?

If you will be working with professional investors who are in the business of buying businesses and are far better at buying businesses than you are at selling them, then you are going to be outgunned for sure. Which is another reason you will want to beef up your side of the negotiating table with a business broker, investment banker, or mergers and acquisitions (M&A) specialist. All too often a business owner will brag about the money they saved in fees because they did the negotiations themselves, when in reality they ended up leaving considerable amounts of money on the table—but they didn't even know it, because of their ignorance.

Why do I say this? Because I help people sell their businesses, and I have sold hundreds of businesses over the years. But when it comes to me selling something of my own, I am almost inept. I fumble and stutter and don't seem to say the right things and get distracted and make all the mistakes an ordinary seller would make. When people are in the process of selling something, especially something of high value and personal to them, they may get a little wacko and not always have good judgment.

One time I was selling a house I owned. I was buying another house, and the purchase of the other house was contingent on my getting my house sold. With the house I was buying, there was a realtor involved, but with the sale of my house, there wasn't, because I was selling it myself. Now, mind you, I have sold a *lot* of stuff. Which would include vehicles, real estate, financial securities, businesses, and so on. By the time I was 18 years old, I had already bought and sold over a dozen cars, so yes, I am experienced at selling. But something happened when I was selling my house. I think, for some reason, part of my brain wasn't working, and I didn't take my own advice.

I didn't follow the process of selling, and I was combative with the buyer, the home inspectors, and everyone involved in the sale. Basically, I was a wacko—and all because I let the sale of the house become so personal that I wasn't thinking right. I had seen this happen before with sellers that I had worked with over the years. I thought they were dum-dums, but I experienced this feeling of being out of control myself, and it was awful.

I am lucky to have gotten the sale of my home completed. I never forgot the helplessness and the feeling of being out of control that I experienced with getting too personal with it. And this is coming from an experienced individual who knows what to do. So, as you can see, I understand why they say, "He who represents himself in a court of law has a fool for a client," because I was that fool!

When attempting to sell something of personal value, you may encounter the following:

1. Your negotiation skills may be skewed because you are too close to the deal since it is of personal value. You will be thinking too much about how the outcome will affect you and not about the transaction. You will lose sight of your goal and, very possibly without knowing it, sabotage yourself in getting the sale completed.

2. You may talk too much. Most sellers talk too much and either relay too much or the wrong kind of information to a buyer, thereby hurting themselves in the long run. Ironically, they think they are disclosing information that the buyer needs, so they just keep talking. I had one very intelligent seller whose leg I actually had to kick under the table to shut up, because he had diarrhea of the mouth and wouldn't stop yakking. He was talking and talking and talking about details of the business that were due diligence items and not pertinent to the sale of the business.

3. You may take all criticism personally and get defensive when the buyers are really just trying to position themselves and see how you react. Nobody likes to hear they have an ugly child. But let go and realize this isn't personal; it's business.

In a sales transaction, two hats are being worn—a buyer's hat and a seller's hat. And they are interchangeable. Sometimes you wear your buyer's hat, and sometimes you wear your seller's hat, but an experienced dealmaker knows these hats need to be worn at the same time for a fair and equitable deal to get done. However, most individuals put their buyer's hat or seller's hat on and try to drive a hard bargain based entirely on the hat they are wearing. It doesn't always work and can cause friction between the two parties. This is when things get personal—when the criticism from one party to another will knock the deal off track, perhaps even to the point where it cannot get back on track again because of the damage caused by the criticism.

4. You could be in an adversarial position from the beginning, meaning they are the buyer, and it is their mission to get the best possible price. Sometimes they will even lie or try to cheat to get the lowest price. You, on the other hand, are the seller, who is trying to get the highest possible price, and therefore you want to remain on the ethical side of the transaction.

Years ago when I started selling businesses professionally, I was working with quite a few new Americans who were first-generation immigrants to the United States. I have a lot of respect for new Americans. It takes courage to leave your home country and immigrate to a foreign country. They want the same thing that our forefathers wanted when they came to America—to have a better life for themselves and their families.

But when it came to negotiating and working to complete a transaction with new Americans, it wasn't working. I was having a terrible time with dismal results, and I couldn't figure out why. It took me about six months before I discovered what the issue was and why we were always in such an adversarial situation, which was cratering quite a few business sales I was working on at the time.

I finally discovered that we were dealing with two different sets of values. You see, I was applying my Midwest values of being very forthright and direct, presenting no-nonsense facts, and meaning what I said. If we agreed upon something, then we were 95% of the way to getting the deal done. But the new Americans I was working with were using the set of values they had grown up with. They loved to negotiate and therefore would throw all sorts of things into the conversation—all as part of the deal—knowing a lot of what they were saying wasn't true.

Here I was with my Midwestern value system, trying to negotiate with new Americans who were using a value system from their home country, which was normal for them. It was a recipe for disaster, and deals just didn't get done until I got it figured out. To get a deal done with individuals from certain countries, I realized that I needed to be a chameleon and apply the same values they were using, instead of relying on my customary Midwest values. Sometimes it takes a little longer to get a deal done, and we still end up at the same place, but by applying the same value system as the new Americans, I was able to keep the deals flowing and eventually close them.

Solution: Hire an intermediary to do the negotiations for you. Even presidents of countries, baseball teams, and large corporations all use intermediaries. So why wouldn't you when you are depending on the best results? Remember, he who represents himself has a fool for a client. Selling your business is probably the single most important financial event of your life. You wouldn't dream of representing yourself in a lawsuit, completing a complex tax return without the assistance of a CPA, or performing surgery on yourself, would you? So why, then, do so many business owners feel they can sell their business without the help of a professional intermediary? They think because they have sold vehicles, properties, and maybe even a business in the past, this makes them competent intermediaries. But it doesn't.

I had one client that I had enjoyed working with for years. One day he called to tell me he'd sold one of his businesses by himself but that he needed my opinion about how to put the deal together. He said selling that one business was one of the hardest things he had ever done, because he wasn't sure what he was doing and was afraid he was missing something. Even though he lucked out on the selling of that first business to an eager and cooperative buyer, he said he didn't want to have anything to do with selling the rest of his companies. He wanted an intermediary. I eventually sold the rest of his businesses, and he was grateful that I did.

Most Business Owners Are Terrible Sellers

"Wow," you might say. "That sounds pretty harsh." Well, I say this because it is easier to buy than it is to sell, as we discussed earlier. Buying is easy, because all you have to do is write a check or come up with the money—and voilà! Transaction done! Plus, we were taught as little kids that if we behaved or did certain chores, then we would be rewarded with some kind of treat or money. So in our minds, we relate buying with something positive and rewarding. It sometimes stimulates a happy feeling and gets the endorphins moving inside us.

On the other hand, selling involves thought, work, and having to perform a task that may or may not be rewarding—and subliminally it doesn't give us the quick gratification we experience from buying. In our minds, buying is fun, rewarding, and gratifying, whereas selling is doing a task, performing work with an unknown timeline as to when it will be gratifying. You get the picture. So beware of this situation, because it is my job to alert you to everything that can go wrong so that you will be aware of these things and not fall into these situations.

Because of this mindset, being a buyer is easy for the same reason that being a seller is hard. As a seller, you are already in possession of what you are selling, and you are comfortable with what you own, and chances are you have owned the business for a long time. I have even had business owners tell me that their business is their baby, and they couldn't sell their business to just anybody. Sorry, but your business is not your baby. It is a business, and its main function is to generate a profit. As I have always said over the years, "Never fall in love with a business or a property, because it can't love you back!"

Now, you may think it is easy for me to say this, because it is not *my* business, and I don't know what you have been through—all the trials and tribulations, as they say. The first time I sold one of my businesses, I took it personally too, but I didn't have someone to explain to me that my business was just that—a business. A business is for producing a profit, and

I would be compensated for selling it. And, by selling the business, it allowed me to move on to a better situation, where I could use the experience and knowledge I had learned from my past business to help me become more successful in my next venture.

So don't get caught in the "business is my baby" syndrome. Keep a clear head, stay focused, and remember that your obligation and goal is to get the highest value from the sale of the business for you and your loved ones, partners, or stockholders.

CHAPTER 5

Know What You Are Selling

BEFORE ANYTHING CAN be bought, sold, or transferred, the buyer and seller must first determine, and then AGREE TO, the intrinsic value of the object. Business transactions are no different.

A Seller's View of Valuation

History and experience tell us that there is usually a difference between the value a buyer places on an object and the value a seller will place on the same object. Therefore, the success, or failure, of any business transaction begins and ends with whether the buyer and seller can find a common value for that object. And that common value is usually somewhere in the middle.

Business owners generally confuse the value of the business with their desire to walk away from the sale with a specific amount of money in their pocket. So they ultimately end up asking a price for the business that is based more on their feelings than on an objective estimate of what the business is worth to a prospective buyer. Or, worse yet, they think in terms of how much money is owed against the business, which has absolutely nothing to do with the value of the business. However, this type of valuation of a business is more common than you might think.

When I first began selling main street businesses such as retail shops, cabinet manufacturers, service companies, and the like, I would begin the valuation process by determining what I thought the business was worth. I would then ask the business owner what they thought it was worth. More than 50% of the time, the business owner's value equaled a little more than what was owed on the business. When I asked them how they came up with such and such price for the business, their response was always that it was how much they needed to pay off the business and have enough money left to relocate, buy another business, or hold them over until they could get a job.

Don't fall into the trap of thinking your business is worth what is owed on it or what it will take to get you out of it and moved on. This idea and the real value of the business are not the same. Be sure you have an intermediary who will be forthcoming and honest about the true market value of your business.

To further complicate matters, there are even subcategories

of buyers and sellers who don't agree among themselves on the value of a business. This is because different types of operators have different business models and overheads; thus, they see different profit pictures. All of this may factor into the value a person will place on a business.

Generally, owners don't know how to arrive at fair market value. Unrealistic owners are the biggest reason why deals fall through. The number-one reason most sales do not get completed is that the seller is unrealistic about the value of their business. Get the facts, and understand the reality of what businesses like yours are selling for in the current market. Never believe anything you read in the trade magazines, or what you may have heard from street talk, as the gospel regarding valuations, because no two situations are the same. Valuations are determined by many different factors.

Fair market value can be defined as "the price a willing seller and a willing buyer, both possessing complete information, agree on when there is no undue pressure to act on either side." And of course, fair market value will be influenced greatly by the economy, availability of financing, and the number of similar businesses for sale in the same market.

We like to say that valuing businesses is like working with Jell-O. It is very hard to get your hands around the business because the business is always changing. A competitor may move in across the street and change the business landscape. Conversely, a competitor may move out and leave you with more customers. Perhaps your city decides to rebuild the road in front of your store. The time it takes for the construction to finish will certainly impact your business.

The most recent example of this type of change is one where the closing of the sale was scheduled for a Friday, and on Thursday, the state highway department showed up and began construction to install a new turn median in front of the business, which closed one of the business entrances. Ultimately, this meant there was an adverse change in the business and the value of the business. This was why the transaction did not close—because the business value changed overnight.

There are many variables to consider in determining the value of a business—too many to list here. The point is nothing stays the same. Change. Change. Change. So what we are searching for is what the business is worth today. Not last year. Not next year when they put in the new subdivision or build a new factory across the street or when a competitor comes out with a new innovational product that changes the landscape of the industry. Think of new entrants, like what Amazon has done to the retail business or how digital media has changed the landscape of magazines and newspapers—and cameras. What is your business worth today?

The value of a business is like a financial statement that a bank has you prepare before it will consider giving you a loan. With a financial statement, the banker learns what you are worth today. Basically, it is a snapshot in today's market of your present value.

You'll need to answer the following questions before you can arrive at the fair market value of your business.

What Do the Numbers Say?

Look at the income and expense numbers for the past three years. Why? Buyers are looking to purchase an income stream and want to see what the business has been doing for at least the past three years. Have the sales numbers been trending up or trending down? All business owners have goals to continually increase sales, thereby increasing the net profit of their business. A successful business will show incremental sales and profitability continually, year after year. However, there are sometimes situations, which a business owner cannot control, that will affect the sales and profitability of the business, stopping the positive trend of increasing sales and profitability.

If you as a business owner have had several years of positive increases in sales and profitability, now is the time if you are considering selling your business. Why? Because if a positive and profitable sales trend is interrupted with a down year in sales and profitability, generally all the explaining in the world to a prospective buyer will not change what has happened. Most buyers will either back off from the purchase of the business or will insist upon a discount of the purchase price because the business appears it may be on its way down.

The moral of the story is this: If you are ever considering selling your business, you want to sell it when the sales numbers and profitability of the business are trending upward. Yes, it is very possible that you could be leaving some upcoming profits on the table, but that is always going to be the case if you are selling a profitable business. Conversely, if you attempt to sell a business that is not trending in a positive direction, you will take a discount because profitability is an unknown going forward. That is why the buyer will want a discount.

Be proactive and sell when the business is profitable and trending up. If you wait until you have a down year and then attempt to sell the business, you will lose the positive momentum and possibly be forced to wait and start over again to achieve another three years of increased sales and profitability before you can achieve the maximum sale price.

KEEP YOUR BOOKS IN ORDER

Profit and loss statements give an indication of the pulse of the business. They give buyers a chance to see if sales have been increasing and if expenses have been consistent. Detailed profit and loss statements are needed. Audited financial statements are the best, with income and expenses audited by an independent accounting firm. Unfortunately, many businesses don't place enough emphasis on making sure their financial statements are detailed and correct. By having audited financial statements, the business has a better chance of getting sold and will often attract a better-quality buyer. It is like the old saying about computers, "Garbage in, garbage out," meaning that if you are not putting the correct financial information into your profit and loss statements, then you are not going to get anything of value out of them.

Lumping sales and expenses into categories without detail is not sufficient. A company owner came to me recently, wanting me to sell their four convenience stores, fuel distribution, bulk plant, corporate offices, trucking, and lubrication business. Although the business was located in a large metropolitan area, a desirable location to many buyers, the owner of the company had no details of his sales and expenses for each of the retail stores and separate divisions of the company. When I asked him why he didn't have the details, he said that was the way they had always done it.

Lumping sales and expenses together for your business is fine if you never expect to sell the business, but the minute you decide to sell, you should begin to get your income and expense numbers in order. The first things that a buyer will want to see are detailed income and expense reports. To make matters worse, the company that lumped all the income and expenses together used an outside accounting firm for years; we're talking here about a business that, if the books and records were in order, would sell in the $10-million-plus range. But by not having good books and records, the business is practically unsalable, unless the seller is willing to take a deep haircut on price. Several millions of dollars lost, all because they did not have good books and records.

You may think this is an isolated incident to which I am referring, but it is really quite common, and I can explain why. If you trace the history back to when many businesses were created, you will realize they were created by entrepreneurs who were creative, found a void in the marketplace, and worked their tails off to make the business successful. Very few of them were knowledgeable or proficient in accounting or in how to keep good books and records. They generally worked out of the checkbook, meaning that if they had money in the checkbook, then they could pay the bills. It is what we call the "cash system"—instead of the accrual form of accounting. Then, as the business progressed and became more successful and financially strong, the owner continued with the same mentality of working out of the checkbook. Only if the entrepreneur was fortunate enough to have an accountant or an accounting firm speak up and suggest that they hire a controller or CFO would the business end up with good books and records.

I know this for a fact. I built a chain of video rental stores from a single store into 155 stores. Along the way, at around 30 to 40 stores, I had the books and records so messed up that I paid Arthur Andersen over $400,000 to get the financials audited and ready for our IPO. And this was in the mid-1990s! It cost me a lot of money to fix my mistake, and I don't know how much money I lost by not having good books and records prior to when I got them fixed.

Having been through the issue of not having good books and records myself, in working with other entrepreneurs, I realized early on that this issue was more common than I originally thought. This is why I have made it my mission to try to connect with a business owner 12 to 24 months prior to them taking their business to market, to help them ensure that they have their books and records in order along with the multitude of other items that need to be addressed before going to market.

As an owner of a business, you need to know exactly where you are making your money and exactly where you are spending your money to achieve maximum profitability. A buyer will need to know these factors too, because sometimes the expenses that are being incurred by the present business owner will not be the same expenses that the next owner is going to incur, making the business more profitable to the new owner than to the present owner.

A good example of this occurs when a business is owned and being operated by a multi-unit operator. A multi-unit operator is one who owns multiple units either around the region or around the country and who has the expense of employing back-office management staff. The employment of the back-office management staff and the additional costs that surround the staff may not be needed or applicable to the new owner. They may already have adequate staff in place within their organization. This factor alone—eliminating the seller's management staff and increasing the profits for the buyer—could very likely increase the sale price of the store by hundreds of thousands of dollars or possibly millions of dollars.

Again, only by providing the profit and loss statements in detail will such an item as management cost be identified, which may possibly increase the sale price of the store. Other expense items that need to be mentioned are personal or non-business-related expense items. Many business owners allocate personal expenses to their business to write off these expenses for tax purposes. Before a business owner shows their profit and loss statements to a prospective buyer, it would greatly behoove them to remove such personal expenses. Remember, if the goal is to get the maximum sale price from the business, then it would be correct to show only the income and expenses that are applicable to that particular business.

There may also be nonrecurring expenses that should be noted. Whether they are capital or expense items, they should be footnoted so that a prospective buyer can understand that these expenses are a one-time event that should not be considered recurring as ordinary expenditures in the daily operations.

SKIMMING MONEY OFF THE BOOKS

What about money that may not have gotten reported on the books—also known as skimming? Well, guess what? The seller doesn't get to claim it twice. If it is not on the seller's financial statements, then they will not get credit for it when it comes time to value the business and cash out.

I encountered one seller who was so proud of what he was skimming that he showed me his little black book that he kept in the top left-hand drawer of his desk. He had kept detailed accounts of all the money he was skimming, which totaled more than $600,000 a year. I refused to represent this individual. I learned later when he sold his business that he thought the $600,000 a year that he was skimming was worth five times the annual amount, or $3 million, as part of the sale price. The buyer held fast and told him that unless he had proof of the $600,000, with solid books and records of where the money came from and when, he was not getting credit for it in the sale price. The seller could not provide good books and records and ended up taking $3 million less for the business.

If you are a business owner and you are skimming cash from the business, stop immediately. I can do the math and show you that the money you believe you are saving in taxes is not as much as you think. In the long run, you will be in a better position by not skimming the money. Plus, it is illegal, and state and federal taxing authorities do not have a sense of humor when it comes to a business owner who has skimmed money from the business.

You may think when I talk about skimming from a business that I am only referring to main street businesses such as mom-and-pops, but that is not the case. Sure, a lot of mom-and-pop businesses skim cash from their dry cleaner, retail store, or restaurant, but I have seen $50 million and $70 million businesses with divisions that deal in cash. The company owners will skim because they think they are saving on taxes, and they like to have some walking-around money in their pocket.

PROPERTY MAINTENANCE

If the property and business have not been kept up-to-date and well maintained, the new owner will have to figure those expenses into their purchase price to bring the assets up to their standards.

There is an old saying, "Pay me now, or pay me later." This is so true. Either the business owner spends the money up front in the form of capital investment to maintain the quality of the assets, or they will pay for it when they decide to sell. The only exception to this rule is if the business owner can sell the property for an alternate use. Then the quality of the asset is not an essential issue.

There are also many situations where franchisors, or city or county inspectors, wait until a business changes hands; then they come in and find a multitude of things that are out-of-date or not in compliance. They hold the buyer and the seller hostage until the items are either corrected or brought up-to-date.

An example would be a franchised hotel where the owner wants to sell. Once they have found a buyer, they must contact the franchisor to make sure the buyer gets approved by the franchisor. At that point, the franchisor will inform the hotel's present owner that for the sale to occur, the hotel needs to be brought up to the current standards of the franchisor's quality control, which may include the need for new beds, furniture, TVs, carpet, and so on. These improvements will often total in the hundreds of thousands of dollars. Somebody has to pay for these improvements or the franchisor is not going to allow the franchise to be transferred to the new owner. It happens in many industries that involve a franchise. This is often the reason you see a hotel that was a Holiday Inn become a Baymont Inn almost overnight, because someone didn't want to pay the money to keep the hotel a Holiday Inn.

But wait. It gets worse. Many times I have seen a restaurant or chain of restaurants—which are operating profitably, doing well, and scoring high with the local health department—decide to sell. A buyer is found, and the buyer and seller have entered into a purchase agreement. The buyer must contact the local health department to get the proper licensing to assume ownership of the restaurants. Since the local health department knows it has some leverage on the business, they suddenly find a multitude of items that are not in compliance with local health standards. Even though the issues they cite have been in place and ongoing for years, and supposedly have been grandfathered in, the health department sees an opportunity to require the restaurant to get up to compliance standards. Is this fair? No, it isn't, but it is a reality. Here again, it is one of many things that need to be researched and addressed before the transfer of a business occurs, regardless of the industry.

Of course, everyone wants to be the big winner in the business deal. The seller wants to get more money for their business than it's actually worth, and the buyer is always looking for an underpriced bargain. However, in my personal experience, the best deals, those with the least amount of trouble from beginning to end, are those with an even "value for price ratio." The deals where the seller received a fair price for what they sold and the buyer received a good value for their investment have always been the fastest and easiest to close, and the longest lasting for the buyer and seller.

Why Get a Market Valuation If You're Not Selling?

Recently I was meeting with a business owner and their chief financial officer, and I expressed my concern about their need for a market valuation of their company. The CFO spoke up and said, "Why do we need to do this when we are not interested in selling our business?" My answer was plain and simple. "Don't you have areas of your business that are underperforming and that should be sold off to allow the capital to be applied to another area of your business, which would give you a higher return on your investment?" His answer was "Yes." Then I said, "Without a market valuation, how will you know what to sell the underperforming portion of your business for?" And the answer is, of course, that they would have no idea.

So it was agreed that the business owner would do a market valuation, knowing it would give them updated information to work with, very possibly helping them sell an underperforming portion of their business and increase the overall value of the company.

A funny side note to this story is that most business owners are their own worst enemies. The CFO and the owner of the business never did get me the profit and loss statements of the businesses. I knew there were several outlets of their business that were not making any money, but they either didn't care they were losing money or were too out of touch with the business to know the urgency of addressing the issue.

You may think this is an isolated issue, but it's not. Many—and I mean *many*—business owners are clueless about their business and don't realize how doing a few things to the business would increase the top-line sales of the business and net profit. I call it the "complacency factor." The business owner becomes either content with the status of the business or complacent in the way they operate the business. Meanwhile the business is not being run in an efficient manner, and there is money either going out the door or not coming in the door because of the owner's complacent attitude.

People forget that, even though they are the company owner and it may be their money, they are still obligated to do the best job they can for the company and its stockholders. If you are a business owner and you are not running the company to your utmost ability, you should treat your position the same as you would the local basketball or baseball coach at the high school. If the local coach is a nice guy or gal, but they continually fail to perform to the standards of the team, what happens? They are replaced with another coach who will utilize the talent of the players and the team.

Your job as a business owner is the same. Your business is your team, the vehicle, the machine that produces the income from which you operate. You may say that you own the company 100% yourself, so therefore you don't have any obligation to any stockholders. But to that I'd say you are incorrect. If you have a family, they are your stockholders. If you don't have a family, then you should be working to improve your employees' performance and lives. Don't ever forget it starts at the top. If you as the owner of the business become complacent, what kind of signal do you think that sends to the rest of the people in the company?

CHAPTER 6

What You Will Need to Get the Sale Done

YOU MUST ASSEMBLE the right team to get the job done. Just as in sports, if a seller doesn't have the right team of players in the game, they will either get defeated or become hurt in some way.

Hire Experts

What is the right team? I propose three important players: (1) an attorney (but not your lifelong golfing buddy) who has experience in business transactions and understands the sale of a business to a buyer; (2) an accountant who understands the tax system, is not afraid to give good tax advice even if that means there's a possibility they will lose your account, and looks out for your best interests; and (3) a seasoned and experienced business intermediary who has working knowledge of how to value businesses and understands the process of selling a privately owned company.

WATCH OUT FOR LEGALMAN AND THE TAXMAN

All too often, a seller gets close to the closing table only to realize they can't afford to sell due to their tax situation. As a seller, you need to know how much your partner "the Taxman" is going to get from the sale first. The Taxman refers to the wide array of federal, state, and local taxes that will need to be paid because of the sale of the business. Taxes generally only occur when a transaction happens, and the sale of a business creates a transaction, so therefore there will be taxes that need to be paid. Remember, it is not always about the sale price of the business but how much you get to put in your pocket when the sale is complete.

Almost all business owners have an attorney, whom we'll call "Legalman," and an accountant they have worked with for years and with whom they feel comfortable working. However—if you play golf with your buddy who is a doctor of general medicine, and you discover you have cancer, you don't have your golfing buddy treat you for cancer, do you? Of course not. You would have your doctor buddy refer you to a specialist in treating the type of cancer you have. Yet for some strange reason, this is not what always happens when it comes to selling a business.

I have worked on transactions valued in the tens of millions of dollars where the seller insisted on using his attorney golfing buddy from the country club to handle the transactional side of the sale. This was despite my urging that he get an attorney with many years of experience in the sale of businesses. Well, you can imagine what happened. My seller was clueless about what was involved in the process of selling, let alone the legal side of the transaction. He ended up leaving hundreds of thousands of dollars on the table because his attorney lacked experience with these kinds of transactions. It got so bad that the buyer's representative called me and said he believed the seller's attorney was incompetent. I told him I knew the seller's attorney was in over his head, but there was nothing I could do about it.

In another situation, the seller's attorney made the seller sign a letter stating the seller wouldn't sue the attorney if the attorney messed up the transaction, because the size of the transaction exceeded his errors and omissions insurance. The attorney had never done a transaction this large. He was nervous about messing something up and getting sued by his client, who had been his client for years. Talk about a vote of confidence from the attorney. Eventually I had to jump in and negotiate with the buyer's attorney, because of the reluctance of the seller's attorney (aka Legalman) to become totally involved in the transaction.

These things really happen. You can't make this stuff up. So be prepared, and make sure you have the right players involved when it comes to the sale of your business.

This is not meant to be a criticism against your attorney,

whom you may have used for many years. The question here is whether your attorney is versed in the sale of businesses. Most attorneys, like doctors, are general practitioners who handle domestic issues like estates, wills, and other general legal matters. They may only do one or two business sale transactions a year, if any. Chances are this is the only time you will sell your business, so make sure you get it done right. Use an attorney who has experience with business sale transactions to handle the legal aspects of the sale.

FIND AN ATTORNEY WHO'S FAMILIAR WITH SELLING BUSINESSES

How do you find the right attorney if you don't think yours is right for the job of selling your business? First, I would start by asking the attorney with whom you have a relationship to refer you to someone they think has the skills and the time to devote to you and the sale of your business.

One business owner I was dealing with did just that. He asked his local attorney (with whom he had worked for years) to refer him to an attorney who was good at business transactions. The local attorney was good at preparing real estate deeds, estates, and divorces, but we were about to enter into a $70-million-plus sale of a business. There was no time to educate a local attorney on how to do business transactions. In other words, we didn't want the local attorney to go to school with my client's business and his money.

Another situation occurred where the seller, against my wishes, decided to use his local attorney to sell his business.

Even though the attorney he had chosen was competent and could perform the needed business transaction, he was strapped for time with his other clients and could not devote the time that was needed to get the sale of the business done. Instead of the process of reaching an agreement and preparing and signing the purchase agreement taking its customary 30 to 45 days, it took five months. This was because the local attorney worked in a small office. One of his partners in the law firm quit, and then an employee quit. The attorney was trying to pick up the additional workload, and as a result he did not have the time to devote to my seller's business transaction, thus delaying the progress of the deal.

Be proactive when employing an attorney and an accountant. Don't settle for just getting by. Chances are you are only going to sell your business one time. You want to make sure it is done correctly and in a timely manner.

Remember, the attorney's role in the selling transaction is to give you legal advice on what can hurt you in the sale, NOT to give you business advice. You are the business owner, and you, not the attorney, built the business into the success it is today. Recently a very successful client of mine, who had enlisted our services to sell his business, decided he needed to ask his attorney a question about a matter. In the conversation, it was brought up that he was selling his business. The attorney basically told him that he thought it was a bad idea, because the business was so profitable. My client made the comment to me later, saying it was easy for the attorney to make such a comment based solely on what he was seeing in the financial statements. The attorney had no idea how much work it was for my client to operate the business and deal with all the issues that go along with the day-to-day operation. He was selling because it had become such a chore to maintain business profitability. My client also knew it was time to sell. The business was trending in the right direction, and he knew the market was right for selling.

FINDING THE RIGHT ACCOUNTANT

I have had the same thing occur with accountants who have worked for the business owner for years. Because they don't want to lose the client's business, the accountant may attempt to sabotage the sale.

Or perhaps the accountant is not in tune with the marketplace in which the business owner operates and throws out a valuation that is nowhere near the market value of the business. This instills a higher value in the business owner's mind, making the owner think the business is worth more than it really is. Unfortunately, this leads to much grief, and there have been times when I have had to be very firm with a business owner and let them know their accountant is wrong about the value of the business. I have sent the business owner back to their accountant to ask them how knowledgeable they are about the industry the seller's business is in, in an attempt to refute his valuation number. Both an accountant and an attorney are needed to make the sale of the business a successful transaction. However, neither of the two are working with buyers every day, and they don't always have an understanding of what businesses are worth or how buyers are reacting to businesses. This is why you want to be represented by an experienced intermediary who does work on the front lines every day, not just on a few occasions in their career.

It probably sounds like I am being cynical. But I share these stories as a warning to business owners in the hope that if they recognize their advisors aren't giving them the proper advice, they won't get further drawn into these situations and they'll be clearheaded and realistic about what's going on. There are so many things that can go wrong when the sale of a business is in process.

Business owners take the daily operation of their business in stride, because they are doing what they have done for years and they feel comfortable in what they do. But they have no idea of the many situations and items lurking in the bushes when it comes time to sell their business. This is because a business has a lot of moving parts. It is not easy to build and operate a business, but it's all too easy to take it for granted. Even the smallest business has many moving parts and should be treated accordingly. Don't let your guard down. Get the right players involved to help you through this difficult and complex process and alert you to things and situations that could hurt you so that you don't get blindsided along the way.

WHAT ABOUT A BUSINESS INTERMEDIARY?

Many people have never heard about a business intermediary. When it comes to having a middleman or someone to facilitate and help with business sale negotiations, especially their own business, it never enters some owners' minds. But a business intermediary is a crucial part of the selling process of your business. A good business intermediary will know the process I have outlined in this book and will help you stay the course and stay focused on your goal, which is to sell your business for the highest value. And since they are generally paid a fee only when the business is sold, they are incentivized too.

So where should you begin in your search to find a business intermediary? One of the best places to start would be with the International Business Brokers Association, which is a group that represents hundreds of business brokers throughout the world. You can find them on the Internet at www.ibba.org.

Know the Legal Makeup of Your Business

Some business owners are not sure what kind of entity they have or what the tax implications are with the entity they own and operate. Realistically, unless you study tax law and stay current, as I have had to do over the years, you would not know this about your business. Tax law is not a thrilling area to read about, and it is constantly changing. If it hasn't changed, the tax people are usually talking about how it may be changing shortly, which only confuses you even more. You end up feeling damned if you sell too soon and damned if you don't sell when you think the tax law is tolerable. But the worst thing you can do is nothing and then end up in a situation where you have to sell when the tax laws are not favorable to your situation. I hope that is why you are reading this book: to find out what you need to be doing before you get into the process of selling your business so that you will have an idea of what to do and what to expect.

Is the business owned by you as a sole proprietor? Are you in a partnership with someone else? Is it a C corporation, an S corporation, or a limited-liability company (LLC)? Determining what type of business you own is an essential first step when thinking about selling your business. Why? Because if you have a partner or are part of a corporation, you may not have the sole legal authority to sell the company. Each corporate structure has a different income tax implication, which may have a profound effect on how much money you put into your pocket when your business is sold.

In today's world, you already have a partner you did not invite to the party. He is the Taxman. He may show up as the state Taxman, the federal Taxman, and possibly a few other Taxmen you didn't even know existed. He will get paid. That is why it is so important to know how your business is set up for tax purposes. If you are a C corp, you will have a different situation when it comes to selling than you will if you are an LLC or an S corp. You need to know this and have a long conversation with your accountant before you get too far down the road in the process of selling. If you don't like what your accountant is telling you, go get a second opinion. Don't ever lose sight of the fact that it is your business, and your money. You want to make sure you get the right advice.

SELLING THROUGH A STOCK SALE

One option that most people do not think about is to do a stock sale, which sells the entire company that owns the business. This currently has capital gains advantages—until the federal government decides to change the tax laws. Without giving any tax advice, let me say that a stock sale enables a person to sell the stock of their company, thus incurring capital gains taxes instead of possibly having to pay tax on ordinary income, which is taxed at a higher rate than capital gains. If you live in a state that has state income taxes, you would also have to pay state income taxes. But a stock sale may, depending on your state, give you dramatic savings in the amount you would have to pay if it were treated as an asset sale.

However, many different factors come into play when making a stock sale. Most attorneys will advise a buyer against doing this type of purchase. I personally have been involved in several stock sales where the buyer got a reduction of the sale price because it was a stock sale, and the seller still came away with more money in their pocket than they would have if they'd done an asset sale. Tax laws can be complex, and with the new tax reforms the federal government is implementing starting in 2018, you will definitely want to investigate what is the best route for you to take—*before* you sell your business, not afterward.

YOUR TAX ACCOUNTANT'S ROLE AND LIMITATIONS

Once you have a general idea about what your business is worth—its fair market value—the next item on the list is to find out your tax exposure. Believe it or not, some people can't afford to sell their own business. Ask your accountant what your tax liability will be when your business is sold.

One of the first things you want to do is sit down with the accountant who is responsible for the tax portion of your business. Generally, the reason people sell businesses is to put as much money into their pocket as possible, or to move the money into another investment. Either way, the goal is to do so with minimal tax consequences.

Remember, the tax accountant's role is to help you with your tax situation—NOT to value your business. I have had many, and I mean many, deals fail to come together because the accountant, who had no experience in the industry in which the business was operating, told the business owner that they thought their business was worth such and such, when in reality the accountant did not have a clue.

Unless your accountant is knowledgeable in business valuations, they will only be able to give you general ideas about what they think your business may be worth based on the historical financial numbers they have reviewed. I have seen all too many times a business owner's trusted and faithful accountant tell their client the business was worth $19 million, when in reality it was only worth, at the top of the market, $13 million. This is because an accountant is working only with the profit and loss statements of the business. Determining the value of the business consists of much more than just the numbers.

There is no way the accountant could know what is going on in your business industry without being involved with that particular industry. Every industry has its ebbs and flows and cycles of ups and downs. Unfortunately, some industries have their downs and don't recover—like the taxi industry contending with Uber in its marketplace. How would you value a taxi company in today's market with the disruption of the industry due to the ride-sharing companies like Uber and Lyft? And we haven't even factored in autonomous driverless cars. Or how would you value an entertainment distribution company with Netflix increasing its creation of in-house content, thereby becoming vertically integrated within the video industry?

These are just a couple of examples. There are similar situations occurring in your business industry. Most accountants would not be aware of these issues and therefore could not give you an accurate idea about what your business is worth.

Remember, it is your business and your money, and you are only going to get one shot at this. We want to make sure we do the best we can to get it right. Don't do what a lot of business owners do and use the SWAG method of valuing their business. Don't know what the SWAG method of valuation is? Scientific Wild-Ass Guess!

CHAPTER 7

There Is a Process to Selling

ARE YOU COMMITTED? Selling a business is a lot of hard work. People don't realize how much work it is to assemble all the data needed for a buyer to get a business sold. Lots of past and present financial and tax records will be needed, along with lists of assets that are to be sold and detailed information regarding the operations of the business—not to mention title work, surveys, purchase agreement issues, and negotiations.

Many transactions fall apart because the seller is either not committed to the process or does not have the mental stamina to continue. The solution is to get help with a seasoned intermediary, someone who will coach you from the beginning to the end so that you are prepared for what is about to happen. In the end, you will be celebrating with a large pot of gold to reward you for many years of hard work and not end up aggravated and empty-handed from not being prepared.

Selling a business reminds me of what a friend of mine said many years ago after he ran a marathon. I remember looking at him and saying, "Wow, you don't look like someone who would be running a marathon."

He responded by saying, "Running a marathon is between the ears. It's more mental than physical."

In other words, you must have the right mindset. And you must have the proper mindset before and during the sale of your business to ensure that you will complete the process.

Focus on the Issues at Hand

One of the things I find myself repeating over and over when I am working with a client is "baby steps, baby steps." By this I am referring to going slowly and not trying to get ahead of the process. Focus only on the issue at hand. I know there are many items that need to be addressed in the selling of a business, but if I were to bring all these items up in the beginning, it would overwhelm the seller and could make them either defensive or depressed thinking about all the things that need to be done.

Occasionally I find myself spoon-feeding the seller, because I don't want them overwhelmed with the entire process. Sure, I will let them know what we will have to do to get the business sold, but we don't have to do everything at one time.

It is best to approach selling your business the same way you would approach eating an elephant. One bite at a time!

Receiving Offers and Closing the Deal

If you've made it to this point, congratulations. You are on the path to selling your business. You have determined a fair market value and prepared yourself for the sale of your business. You either employed the services of an intermediary or decided to sell the business on your own. And after marketing your business to potential buyers, you will be getting an offer to purchase. And the potential buyer may be a serious candidate. What happens now?

THE OFFER

Your serious buyer will make you an offer in writing. Offers can come in a few different forms. The only offers I ever take seriously are those I get in writing with a signature. Verbal offers are like having a conversation, but they are not real offers. Real offers come in the form of a written offer with an escrow check.

Written offers will generally come in two basic forms: a "letter of intent" or a "purchase agreement." Both documents are essentially an offer to purchase a business, with the exception that a letter of intent is usually nonbinding. It is sometimes used by a buyer to gain some confidential information before a total commitment is made.

The letter of intent is used as a precursor to the purchase

agreement. The reason a buyer would present a letter of intent is to get a deeper understanding of the seller's business and have the opportunity to review the seller's books and records. A letter of intent is also used to see if the buyer and seller can agree in principle to price and terms before a formal purchase agreement is written up. If the buyer and seller can't agree on price and terms up front, there is no reason to prepare a purchase agreement.

Also, there will be some disclaimers in a letter of intent and certain items the buyer is looking to verify before moving to a purchase agreement. There is usually a "No Shop" clause in a letter of intent, stating that while the letter of intent is in effect, the seller must take his business off the market and not talk with other possible buyers. But the main purpose of a letter of intent is to get the buyer and seller to agree on the price and terms of the sale of the business.

Once the buyer has had a chance to review some general numbers pertaining to the books and records of the business and has found them to be satisfactory, and the buyer and seller have agreed on the price and terms of the sale, a formal purchase agreement will be prepared.

Should you ask for an escrow check when you are presented with a letter of intent? That's up to you, but I like to see the buyer have some skin in the game, even if the offer is nonbinding. If you do, make sure to have the buyer make the check payable to your attorney or a title company to be held in escrow.

Earlier I mentioned that in one situation it took the buyer and seller five months to negotiate a purchase agreement.

This is too long. Most of the time you can expect the buyer to present the seller with a purchase agreement within 30 to 60 days and sometimes sooner, depending on the complexity of the business being sold. Keep in mind that whoever prepares the purchase agreement will prepare it in their favor. If you think I am kidding about this, you are dead wrong.

One of the things I learned early on with my legal training was that you always want to be the one who prepares the agreement, because there are certain items that you want to make sure are in the agreement that protect your interests.

Whenever I am in the process of buying a property or a business, I offer to prepare the paperwork. I will then contact the attorney I have decided to use, based on the kind of transaction it is, to prepare either a buyer's agreement or a seller's agreement, depending on which side of the transaction I am on. This is common practice. If you don't play in this area of purchase and sale transactions, you might not know this.

Remember the purchase agreement that took five months to get signed? Well, part of the reason it took so long was that the buyer prepared the agreement and had a multitude of items in the agreement that were not pertinent to the transaction. The seller's attorney had to spend excessive time removing these items and then arguing with the buyer's attorney, who didn't want those items taken out.

An attorney told me one time that you never want to be the only attorney in town, because if you are, you don't have anybody to argue with. Attorneys get paid for arguing with another attorney.

There are different kinds of agreements, and whoever is

the one preparing the agreement will either put additional items in the agreement to protect their client or they will leave out certain items to shield their client from certain warranties or issues that may arise.

Now that we have an offer and a signed purchase agreement, we can consider ourselves on first base. But we have a long way to go, and now the game gets interesting.

DUE DILIGENCE

"Due diligence" is the time between the signing of the purchase agreement and the final closing. During this time, to verify their purchase decision, the buyer is responsible for verifying all the information the seller provided the buyer. Your responsibility as a seller is to be honest and provide accurate information in a timely manner.

I believe the due diligence part of selling your business is the hardest part of the selling process, because as a seller you know your business inside and out. You may have started your business. You probably know where every piece of paper is and why you have certain equipment or assets stuck in some corner. You built the business, and it has been your life for years.

But the buyer doesn't know a thing about your business. They may have looked at some financial statements and taken a tour of the facilities, but that's about it. So they need to get up to speed. They are going to ask you for lots of information and paperwork you haven't looked at for years.

During due diligence, you will need to keep your cool and

not get stressed out or upset. I had one seller who was working so hard during the due diligence process that his wife thought he was going to have a heart attack because of the stress of having to find the information the buyer needed. Ironically, he was selling the business because his family members had a history of having heart attacks in their 60s.

Another seller became combative and hostile with the buyer, complaining that the items the buyer was asking for were frivolous and not needed. He was wrong; the buyer did need the requested items. But the seller was not prepared when it came to selling his business, which in turn created more stress than was needed.

Due diligence is generally where the deal will fall apart, if it is going to fall apart at all. The buyer is digging around in all parts of your business, and they have the right to do so. They need to know what they are buying. All too often the owner of the business has a selective memory. He has forgotten to tell the intermediary, and/or the buyer, about certain things regarding the business that will come out during the due diligence period. You must be careful as a seller during the due diligence process not to take things personally. Remember, the buyer is about to spend a large amount of money and make a big financial decision. They are concerned about making sure they know what they are getting into. So it pays to put yourself in the buyer's shoes and look at the purchase transaction from the buyer's point of view.

It may also slip the seller's mind to share with the intermediary or the buyer about certain employment contracts that are in place with some key employees, or the fact that the employee contracts have expired. Nobody ever took the time to sit down and renew them, and now they are thinking about selling the business and don't have the key employees they thought they had. Or it may be the service contracts or vendor contracts you have in place; these could impact the financial future for the buyer, who is not expecting to have any restraints when they take over the business. Or worse yet, it could be the first-right-to-purchase (right of first refusal) option that may be built into a vendor or franchisor agreement. And I have not even touched on the various liens from federal or state agencies that may exist, or old UCCs that are lurking in the weeds, which will arise when property title work is done.

A UCC filing refers to the UCC-1 Financing Statement, which is a legal form that a creditor files to give notice that it has or might have an interest in the personal or business property of a debtor. In exchange, the small business will obtain a loan. Creditors are quick to file such a form when a loan is made but quite often are lax and forgetful in removing them after the loan has been paid.

What generally happens is that after the loan has been paid off, the vendor or bank fails to file a release of the UCC, even though they are supposed to. The release never gets filed, and many years can pass. The vendor has gone out of business and/or the bank has been purchased by another bank, and here you are, stuck with this UCC on file against your business—causing you to have to track down the people who can sign a release. This usually happens just before closing, because the seller wasn't aware of anything like this.

I have seen situations where the amount of the UCC lien forced the sale to be postponed. That's why it's called due diligence. Your business is going to get a good look-over by the buyer. This is why I am suggesting that, as a prudent seller, you should do your own due diligence before you engage with a buyer. Don't wait until you have a buyer, when you are in a reactionary mode. This could very possibly cost you the sale of the business.

KEEPING CALM DURING DUE DILIGENCE

My goal is to prepare the owner of the business for what will happen in the sales process. I coach them through the process to reduce stress so everything can flow smoothly. What you don't want are surprises halfway through the selling process. If there is going to be an issue, it usually occurs during the due diligence period. Here again, you want to be prepared. You are not expected to know about all of this unless you have been through the process of selling your business at an earlier time.

I remember the first time I went through the due diligence process. I was the seller, and I was selling to a major company. I was overwhelmed. I had built a company that had over a couple hundred employees and about 50 locations. The due diligence process was brutal, because I was alone. I still remember the buyer presenting me with their due diligence list of items they wanted from me. I took the requests and the list of due diligence items personally and got defensive, angry, and emotional. After I understood *why* the buyer wanted to review the information they had requested, I calmed down.

At first blush, you, the seller, might think you're being insulted by the buyer. You consider yourself to be an honest individual who would not try to hide anything or pull something over on the buyer. But once you realize it isn't personal and the buyer is required either by their stockholders, partners, or (definitely) their lender to inspect the business using a due diligence list, then you can relax and know that you would want to do the same thing.

SELLING MY FIRST BUSINESS—WITHOUT EXPERT HELP

I didn't have an intermediary to assist me the first time I sold my business, but I wish I had. Back then I didn't know that there were intermediaries who could help in the process of selling your business. Plus, to make matters worse, I had already been approached by a buyer who wanted to buy my business. Not knowing the process of how to work with a buyer on a large scale was not good for me. I was ignorant about how to deal with the buyer, because I was unprepared to sell a multimillion-dollar business to an experienced buyer.

Mind you, I was smart about how to run my business. I had built the business from nothing into a national retail and distribution business. I was well known in the industry and in the top 25 of my business category in the United States—and still growing. I had bought and sold probably 10 to 15 businesses by then, so I thought I was pretty sharp at business. However, I was wrong. I may have known what I was doing when it came to operating my business and buying and selling businesses from other businesspeople like myself, but I was unprepared for the sale of my business to a financial buyer—and it cost me dearly.

When I say "financial buyer," I am referring to someone who has worked previously in mergers and acquisitions or in the financial world, where they've taken other people's money and invested it to get a favorable return, as a private equity group does. These buyers are willing to invest money into the purchase of a business, but they need to get a certain return on their investment or they're not interested. It's all about the numbers. They are not interested in the touchy-feely part of the business or how attached you may be to it or how you have worked your entire life building the business. For them, it's only about the numbers.

I was not just unprepared, but I also had no one who could help me. I tried talking to my accountant. Even though he was a good accountant and had done my profit and loss statements for years and filed my taxes, he was clueless on market valuation and what I should do. All he could do was crank out past profit and loss statements and provide copies of old tax returns for the due diligence. And my attorney, who was also a minority partner in my business, was not able to help either. He was an attorney who worked on wills and estates and local real estate deals. The sale of a business of the size I had created was foreign to him and over his head, and he admitted it.

So here I was with no backup team to help me through the selling process. I am sure you are thinking at this point: If you didn't have anyone to help you through the process of selling the business, why didn't you stop the sale and go get help?

Well, I couldn't. Because the business was growing so fast, I had many orders, but I was running out of money even though the business was profitable. I had waited too long to assemble my team of players and had gotten myself in a jam. I needed the money—or many people would be losing their jobs. I would have been OK, but I didn't want the people who had helped me build the business to lose their jobs. It was either lay a lot of people off and quit growing the business or sell the business and let the next person take it to a higher level, which would protect the people and allow them to keep their jobs. That is what I did.

However, not knowing the process and what to expect in the sale of my business was brutal and expensive for me. I left money on the table because of not being prepared and not having the right people in place to help me through the process. I never forgot the horrible and lost feelings I had during the due diligence process, wondering what I could have done differently and how I could get this over with.

So, when I work with a client on selling their business, they are not only getting the experience of someone who has done the process of selling a business hundreds of times, including selling my own businesses. They're also getting someone who knows what that stress feels like in the bottom of my stomach, and I can empathize with them. It is what I call being able to offer my "expensive experience."

I am fortunate that I got the deal done without going nuts. But then I was in my early 40s, had more energy, and didn't know any better. Sometimes it pays to be young and foolish, but if you are in your 60s or beyond, I have found that things don't roll off your back quite as easily as they did when you were younger. And selling your business at a later age is more serious, because you know that chances are you are only going to get one shot at the sales process, and you want to be sure you get it done right.

Someone once said to me that it is OK to be young and broke, because you think you are going to live forever and think you have all the time in the world to make money. But you don't want to be old and broke, because when you get older, you realize that you are not going to live forever, and you only have a limited amount of time to get the money back!

To give you an idea of what will be expected of you in due diligence, I have included a general sample list. Depending on the industry your business is in, the due diligence list can be much longer and more detailed than what is shown in the following example.

I realize the list can be intimidating. However, remember the buyer knows very little about your business, and you know everything about your business. You have lived it and know the ins and outs of it. So you shouldn't be surprised that the buyer will have many questions in the due diligence review. The buyer is simply asking for you to prove to them that what you represented in the selling process is what you really are selling them. As I mentioned earlier, the Boy Scouts have a motto for this: "Be prepared."

Sample Due Diligence Checklist

1. Organization and Good Standing
   - ✓ The company's articles of incorporation and all amendments
   - ✓ A certificate of good standing from the secretary of state of the state where the company is incorporated

2. Financial Information
   - ✓ The most recent audited profit and loss statements for the past three years and year-to-date. If not audited, then unaudited profit and loss statements for the past three years and year-to-date
   - ✓ A schedule of inventory
   - ✓ Historical capital expenditures (3 years)
   - ✓ Insurance loss runs—general liability (3 years)

3. Physical Assets
   - ✓ A schedule of fixed assets
   - ✓ All UCC filings
   - ✓ All leases of equipment

4. Real Estate
   - ✓ Copies of all real estate leases, deeds, mortgages, title policies, surveys, zoning approvals, variances, or use permits

5. Employees and Employee Benefits

   ✓ A list of employees, including positions, current salaries, salaries and bonuses paid during past three years, and years of service

   ✓ Employee contracts and/or independent contractor agreements

   ✓ The company's personnel handbook and a schedule of all employee benefits and holiday, vacation, and sick leave policies

   ✓ A list and description of benefits of all employee health and welfare insurance policies or self-funded arrangements

   ✓ A description of workers' compensation claim history

6. Licenses and Permits

   ✓ Copies of any governmental, state, or local licenses, permits, or consents

   ✓ Any correspondence or documents relating to any proceedings of any regulatory agency

7. Environmental Issues, Licenses, Permits

   ✓ Environmental audits, if any

   ✓ A list of environmental permits and licenses

   ✓ A list identifying and describing any environmental litigation or investigations

   ✓ A list identifying and describing any contingent environmental liabilities or continuing indemnification obligations

8. Taxes

   ✓ Federal, state, local, and foreign income tax returns for the past three years

   ✓ State sales tax returns for the past two years

   ✓ Any tax liens

9. Material Contracts

   ✓ Any distribution agreements, sales representative agreements, marketing agreements, and supply agreements

   ✓ All other material contracts

10. Customer Information

   ✓ Any supply or service agreements

   ✓ List of customers who may have credit accounts with the company

   ✓ A list of aging accounts showing how much each customer owes and how timely they pay

   ✓ The company's current advertising programs, marketing plans, budgets, and printed marketing materials

   ✓ A description of the company's major competitors

11. Litigation

   ✓ A schedule of all pending litigation

   ✓ A description of any threatened litigation

   ✓ Documents relating to any injunctions, consent

decrees, or settlements to which the company
is a party

✓ A list of unsatisfied judgments

12. Insurance Coverage

✓ A schedule and copies of the company's general
liability, personal and real property, product liability,
errors and omissions, key-man, directors and officers,
workers' compensation, and other insurance

CLOSING THE DEAL

You will need an attorney or title company to help in preparing the needed documents. These include, but are not limited to, the following: asset purchase agreement, escrow agreement, bill of sale, equipment list, various releases, assignments, deeds, indemnification forms, employee information, service contracts, and other documents.

These are standard items that will be covered by your attorney, along with a list of other disclosures and various required documents.

The listed due diligence documents are of the least concern to you when it comes to the closing. The closer you get to the closing date, the more you'll find yourself experiencing additional anxiety—and counting down the days and wondering what could possibly go wrong that could stop or delay the closing. I am not a worrier, but when it comes to closings, I begin to get concerned, and as a seller, you should too.

There are many things that can go awry before the closing.

Of course, there are the usual things that will come up, like title issues, liens, and lenders wanting certain releases and documents signed that indemnify each other, to list a few. These types of items are not uncommon, and in my world, they're to be expected. The types of things I get concerned about are the ones I don't have any control over. Title issues, bad easements, and environmental issues can all be solved with money. As I mentioned earlier, I learned many years ago: If an issue can be solved with money, then it is not a problem. (If you don't think this is true, think about having a bad medical problem and knowing money isn't going to solve it.)

The things that keep me up at night are all part of the Dismal D's, which you may recall from our list in chapter 2 of reasons for selling a business. These are—

- Death
- Disease
- Divorce
- Disaster
- Distraction
- Debt
- Delusion
- Disinterest
- Declining sales
- Dissention among partners
- Disruptive and aggressive competition in the marketplace
- And my favorite one, Dumb

One time when we were getting ready to close a very large transaction, the seller's wife ran off with one of their vendors and demanded a divorce. This was during the due diligence period, and we were only 45 days from closing. Luckily, we offered and were able to get the wife to sign a release and pay her off from the closing to get the deal done. We were all sitting on the edge of our seats, wondering what the wife's demands would be.

Another time the seller was in deeper financial trouble than we realized. The bank shut off his credit line and began foreclosure proceedings. The seller had broken the covenants of his loan agreement, and the bank wanted its money *now*, not later. Without a credit line, the business's ability to operate was basically shut off, and the seller was forced to sell off parts of the business to keep it afloat. Whereas before we'd expected to have the entire business sold for a large amount of money, instead the seller had to do multiple transactions to get the business sold—and for a lot less money.

On more than one occasion during due diligence, the buyer found a discrepancy in the seller's books and records showing the sales were not as they had been presented, thereby reducing the net profit of the company. Either the sale did not go through or the seller ended up reducing the purchase price of his business.

On other occasions during due diligence, a competitor either came into the marketplace or was in the marketplace, and the seller failed to disclose this to the buyer. I had this happen when the buyer was from another state. I asked the seller if there was any direct competition, and the seller replied no, there wasn't any. When the buyer came to do a physical inspection of the business, he found a direct competitor who had been in the marketplace for six months, which the seller had not disclosed. The seller lost all credibility with the buyer, and the buyer terminated the transaction.

There have been times when a partner would refuse to sell, thereby stopping the sale of the business. When the partner is a family member, it's even worse. If the business is multigenerational, there have been times when the dad and the kids want to sell the business, but the grandparents who started the business are still alive, and they end up killing the deal, even though it was already in due diligence.

And there have been too many times when the sellers are reluctant sellers, and they end up becoming hostile and fighting over every little detail, thus aggravating the buyer to the point that they say, "Forget it," and walk away. This one falls under "Dumb," and it happens more often than you would think. Don't let this be you!

Yet another time we were scheduled to close on Friday at 1:00 p.m., and the company had a considerable amount of inventory that needed to be counted. The inventory was done Wednesday so that all the numbers could be included in the closing statement. The business had been owned by the same family for 40 years, and the owner was selling it to retire with his wife after many years of operation.

On Thursday morning, I got a call from an individual who worked for American Business Brokers & Advisors (ABBA), who was overseeing the transaction, to tell me how things were going. The sale was on track to close on Friday. But on

Thursday afternoon I got another call from my ABBA guy. "You're not going to believe what just happened," he said. He was frantic, stuttering, and going on until I asked him what the problem was. He said we were 18 hours from closing, and the seller had just died!

Yes, this is one of the Dismal D's I keep referring to. Fortunately, the seller must have known he had some health issues and was prudent about having given a signed power of attorney to his wife. All other documents were in their names together as joint tenants, so the wife was able to step in and complete the closing and the sale of the business.

I believe in momentum; once you get a process started, you don't want to stop or slow down. You keep the momentum going, and you focus on the finish line. That is why I object anytime an attorney, title company, vendor, or anyone who is involved in the closing process wants to delay or postpone the process.

Not only do we lose time but we also lose momentum from many different people—and the mindset can become "Oh, well, we will just hold off for a little while on this issue." Then it happens again and again, and if you are not careful, the deal will fall apart, and nobody will realize what happened.

CHAPTER 8

How Long Does It Take to Sell a Business?

TO BEGIN WITH, the one thing a seller needs more than anything else when selling their business is PATIENCE. You must be patient in the negotiations. You must be patient with the prospective buyers. You must be patient with the requests for information from buyers and their lenders. You must be patient with your business intermediary. And most of all, you must have patience with your family, because they will hear all your frustration and aggravation that may surface during the process of selling your business.

One of my sellers called me recently. He told me his wife and daughter had gone on a five-day trip, and he was home by himself, dog-sitting. I thought that sounded restful. A couple of days later, when the due diligence requests from the buyer had heated up, he called me, cussing; he was an emotional wreck. He was beside himself, having a hard time controlling his emotions over some items that the buyer was requesting. As usual, I listened to him and calmed him down. We walked through the list of items and why the buyer needed them. He was OK with everything. Then at the end of the conversation, he said he was glad I was there for him to talk to, as otherwise he would be venting all his frustrations to his wife.

As I listened, I thought to myself, *This is what I do for a living—it's not just the financial and business expertise I offer; it's the emotional support.* I am used to these types of issues, and I know how to deal with them; on the other hand, his family is not the right outlet for his stress. (And this guy was stressed to the gills!) Sometimes I worry about family members, especially spouses, when there's a lot of stress around selling a business. So that's why I remind my clients: Please have patience with everyone. Things will get done. Take baby steps.

Most importantly, be patient with yourself. If you have never sold a business before, you won't know about the level of distraction and time demanded from you and the mental strain necessary to maintain focus through the selling process.

Sellers fail to realize that selling a business is a process and not an event. The process of selling your business has many stages. It is easy to become frustrated with all the time and energy it takes.

SELLING TIMELINES

Selling a business involves a structured process that takes time—overall, between 6 and 12 months from inception to closing, and this is *after* you have connected with a qualified buyer. I am not counting the amount of time needed before you sell the business.

As I've said earlier, as a broker I like to engage with a business owner 12 to 24 months before they sell their business; this is primarily to help them prepare the business for sale. During this time, there will be many items and issues that will need to be addressed, all requiring time and effort. Once the tasks on the timeline have been accomplished, a seller is ready to go forward with selling their business.

Timeline Tasks

- Decide to sell your business.
- Find a business broker or investment banker who has experience and knowledge of working in the same industry as your business (30 days).
- Determine the market value of your business (2 to 4 weeks).
- Meet with a tax accountant to assess possible taxes that will need to be paid (2 to 4 weeks).
- Marketing package prepared by business broker or investment banker (3 to 4 weeks).

- Place business on the market for sale and begin search for buyer (30 to 180 days to find a buyer).

- Negotiate letter of intent to determine the selling price and terms (two weeks).

- Buyer presents seller with purchase contract (30 to 60 days to consummate).

- Buyer begins due diligence process (30 to 90 days).

- Transition period (30 days).

- Close on sale of business.

PUT YOUR TEAM TOGETHER

Next, you will be putting your team together. By "your team," I am including whoever will be helping you within your office to locate and obtain the necessary documents needed for the sale of the business. Then you will have to decide what attorney, accountant, and intermediary you are going to use. It sounds simple enough, but again, you want to make sure you have the right players on your team; you may end up having to interview multiple individuals to find the ones with whom you want to work.

Once you have selected your team, you will need to engage each of them and find out how much time they will need to do their part of the job. You may find the accountant you want to use, and they will say they can't work on the sale of your business now, because they are in tax season. They will want you to wait until they are not so busy. An attorney may say they have several court cases they are in the process of dealing with and would like for you to wait until they are finished with them. A business intermediary may not be available either, because they are tied up with other transactions that have reached the crucial stage of the transaction. Again, you want to work on your timeline and not be put off by the other parties, but remember you need all three of these individuals for the sale to go as smoothly as possible.

The amount of time involved in team selecting could be up to six months. The business intermediary will need three to four weeks, depending on the size and complexity of the business, to put the marketing package together.

FIND YOUR BUYER

The amount of time it takes to find a buyer will depend on what kind of business intermediary you use and whether the business is put up for bid or buyers are solicited individually. You should expect the process to find a buyer to take one to six months, depending on what the market is like for the type of business you are selling. Sometimes it takes a year to find a buyer. You may find a buyer, but during the process the deal may fall through and put you back to square one. I have found over the years that frequently the first buyer is not the one who ends up buying the business. The first buyer may get the seller to agree on price and terms, and then during due diligence, the deal falls through. But the seller has gotten his mind partway around how the selling process is supposed to work, and a lot of the due diligence work is done. So the next buyer is the one who reaps the rewards and gets the deal closed.

PREPARE THE PURCHASE AGREEMENT

After the buyer has been engaged, there's still the process of preparing the purchase agreement, getting it signed, and due diligence. For these items, we should allocate between 30 and 60 days for the purchase agreement and between 30 and 90 days for due diligence.

Next is the transition period, where the buyer and the seller have agreed to go forward with the transaction. The escrow money goes hard, and everyone is working toward closing. Figure about 30 days for this time period.

CLOSING DATE

Now we are at the closing date. All the due diligence is done, the buyer has the money, and it is about to be transferred to the escrow agent. All the documents have been signed, and we are just waiting for . . . what?

That's right—what are we waiting for? There is always *something* that either the buyer or the seller is waiting for to get the deal closed; here again, this is reality. There generally will be something that was outstanding or forgotten, or a third party will come out of the woodwork with something that is needed.

For example, one week before closing a large transaction, the buyer's lender called him and said they needed detailed environmental documentation on a part of the business the buyer was purchasing. This was after the lead loan officer for the bank had told them everything was good to go and there were no outstanding issues. Luckily, the buyer was able to get the requested documentation to the lender, and the deal closed on time.

Caution: Attorneys and lenders always like to ask for extensions to closing. Many attorneys want to make sure everything is perfect before closing, and they are used to asking the judge for an extension—because either they don't have their work done or the timeline doesn't coincide with their schedule.

Don't let yourself fall into this trap. You may think I'm exaggerating, but I'm not. There have been many times where if the seller had not spoken up, based on my coaching to get the transaction closed, it would have taken much longer. And there is always the possibility that the transaction will never close, because of the Dismal D's. Am I being cynical? Yes. And it is only because of my experience, having seen what can happen and what very well might happen. So, when you have a closing date set, work for that date and don't back off.

And here's another caution: Do not set the closing day on a Monday or a Friday, because on Mondays people are trying to fix what work didn't get done over the weekend, and they're likely to be distracted. They may hurry though the documents and miss something. Fridays are bad too, because if there's something missing that's needed for the closing, it is too easy for the parties to put off the closing till Monday. That just makes more time for one of the Dismal D's to rear its ugly head.

Timelines, Revisited

If you are just starting the process and have not connected with a buyer, then the selling process could take years until you find the right buyer who's financially qualified. It is a very detailed process, and not all sellers are up to accomplishing it without guidance from a trained professional who's performed this process many times before.

And when I say 6 to 12 months, that's a quick timeline. I am not including all the different things that can and usually do happen during the selling process.

Most sellers tell me that everything will be all right: Their business is clean, and there will not be any issues. Too often I find out later that their business is actually a cluttered mess with title issues, easement problems, commingled assets, family friction, and domestic disputes. So, unless you have audited statements and have been staying current on keeping personal expenses out of the business, chances are it will take longer than 6 to 12 months to sell your business.

I have always believed that if I could sit and talk with the owner of a business 12 to 24 months before they decide to sell their business, I could help them understand what it will take to prepare themselves and their business to be sold and guide them in the right direction.

Some business owners say, "Oh, I know my business is in good shape. I will work with my accountant and attorney, so things will be fine." But let me ask you this: Who would *you* rather be talking to when it comes to selling your business? Remember that your business is probably the biggest financial asset you own, the resource you will draw on to retire and enjoy your golden years. Do you want to be talking to an accountant/CPA who has never sold a business? Or would you rather talk to someone who makes their living working with business owners every day, preparing them and coaching them through the sale process—a professional, who has done hundreds of sales transactions and is on the front lines working with buyers and sellers every day?

Everyone wants the process of selling their business to go smoothly and accomplish the ultimate—a closing with the owner getting the maximum amount of money in their pocket, done with the least amount of stress possible. The best way to accomplish this is to plan and begin early by preparing the business for sale. And by preparing you, the seller, so that you are in the proper mindset, ready to invest the time and effort it will take to accomplish your goal of selling.

On a final note, let me say this again: Of all the businesses I have sold, and they are in the hundreds, I cannot remember one seller who has come back to me and said they wished they had not sold their business. I have had some business owners tell me the only regret they had was that they didn't sell the business sooner, but none ever regretted selling.

Good luck and enjoy the journey. Remember the old Chinese saying: "The journey of a thousand miles begins with the first step."

Conclusion

NOBODY LIKES TO think about selling their business. For some people, it is like the thought of having to buy a burial plot. But someday your business will be for sale.

You can hope the sale occurs while you are still alive, but the sale may occur after you have passed away. Regardless, the business will eventually be sold. If not by you, then by your relatives.

Preparing for the Inevitable

Most business owners I have worked with are very much in control of their business, and because of that control, their business has been a success. Because of this control, most of the business owners I have worked with decide early on whether there is a family member who will succeed them and continue to operate the business. If there is no family member, and they want to control the destiny of the business, they sell it while they are alive and still in control.

A recent example of this was when the owner of a large transportation company contacted me about valuing the company he was considering selling. The owner was a third-generation owner. He had his son working with him in the business, too, which made this business a fourth-generation business. It is very unusual for a business to go four generations. But the owner had the courage and insight to recognize that even though his son worked in the daily operations of the business, he didn't have the mental aptitude or ability to continue the business on a successful path, let alone take the business to the next level.

We sold the entire business at a great profit, which allowed the owner to retire and financially fund his son in a new and different business venture that was more suited to his ability and personality.

Many times business owners tell me they are tired of the operational hassle of running the business. They say they will become chairman of the company and still enjoy the profits from the business but that they are going to hire a professional manager to operate it.

Unfortunately, my advice has always been the same: It won't work. I am not trying to be negative. There is a possibility that it will work. But my experience over the years is that if you are a business owner who has been operating your business with 100% control and have been able to do what you want, then there is no way you will be able to step aside, let someone from the outside operate your business, and put yourself in second place.

It would drive you crazy to give up control. All you would do is meddle in the business and criticize the individual who is trying to learn about the business and operate it on an efficient level. Not to mention all the changes the new manager would make. You may think you wouldn't let them make a lot of changes, because you'd be there to guide them. But really, who are you kidding? If you built the business over the years and have control-freak tendencies, you are not going to change now just because you are getting tired and burned out. Face the facts. Be realistic with yourself and admit when it is time to move on.

Having been an old operator and messing up so many things in my business, there is one thing that I have learned over the years, and that is to analyze every deal I get involved in. When things were not moving as smoothly as I would have liked, I tried to determine who or what common denominator was causing the issues. And sometimes, I discovered that the common denominator causing the problem was *me*!

Yes, I was the problem. I had to either take myself out of the deal or go into a dark room, sit down, and have a talk with myself to get things straightened out. I think in the psychology textbooks this is called "being accountable for your actions." That is what I am referring to if you think you are going to hire a manager to oversee and operate the company while you sit on the sidelines and try to live the good life.

The same thing applies to family members, too, because they grew up in the business while Mom and Dad built the business, but the business wasn't their dream. It was there for them and helped provide for their schooling and their upbringing. Sure, one of the kids might migrate to the business, but they will never have the same attachment to it as the founders. This is one reason why it is so rare to see multi-generational businesses continue to be in business.

Research shows us that approximately 30% of all family-owned businesses survive into the second generation, and only 12% survive into the third generation. Surprisingly, only 3% of all family businesses operate in the fourth generation and beyond. Making it to the fourth generation is very rare! Of the 70% of businesses that fail to transition successfully, 60% fail due to problems with communication and trust, 25% fail due to a lack of preparation by the next generation, and 15% fail from all other issues (e.g., poor tax or financial planning, legal advice, etc.). Therefore, roughly 85% of business transitions fail due to a lack of communication, trust, or next-generation competency.

An article in the July 2013 issue of *Forbes* magazine, "The Facts of Family Business," said it all when describing family businesses and their survival: "Family businesses generate over 50% of the US gross national product (GNP), but less than one-third of family businesses survive the transition from first- to second-generation ownership. Another 50% don't survive the transition from second to third generation.

"From Berkshire Hathaway and Wal-Mart Stores Inc. to small stores everywhere, about 90% of all US businesses are family owned or are controlled by a family. The biggest issue with many family businesses is that they get stuck doing things the same way they have for years, even when the business outgrows that structure. The founding generation holds on to the reins of leadership too long and won't pass control to their children.

"What makes it even more difficult is that the company's hierarchy typically reflects the family's pecking order, regardless of what the organization chart says. Each family member plays the same role inside their company. For example, the bully brother is the same bully in the business, forcing everyone to do it his way. Whoever is the head of the household wants to tell everyone else what to do. The peacemaker in the family tries to smooth things over when tempers explode. The mothering type who controls the budget at home now wants to approve how every dollar is spent at the business.

"Family businesses only change when the pain is so great that they can't stay where they are. Sometimes this is not only tearing their company apart but their personal lives as well. When this happens, the family has four choices:

1. Sell the business.
2. Merge the business.
3. Shut the business down.
4. Stay the same.

"If they decide to stay the same, these are the key questions they then must answer:

1. Do they all stay in this business together or does someone exit?

2. Is it time for the senior generation to pass the company on to the next one?

3. Do they bring in a professional manager?

"For family businesses that are rooted in tradition, the most difficult part of the decision is to actually implement a change that will lead to a more profitable and happier business."

Change is what selling your business is all about—and change is very difficult for many people. That is why I want to reiterate: Most people, especially men, do not like change and therefore will generally wait too long to implement any type of change.

If you think I am overstating or kidding about this type of behavior, take the common denominator test I referred to earlier. Go sit by yourself. Be honest with yourself, and examine whether you are receptive to change. I admit that I am not. I like to keep things the way they are. I like eating the same foods, having the same items in the refrigerator, going to the same places for vacation, and hanging out with the same people. I admit this because many men I have talked to over the years have told me they feel the same way, and their wives complain about how boring their husbands are because they don't like change. They read the same papers every day and stick to the same routines.

There is a chance that the business will be sold to an insider, such as a relative or family member. It might be somebody outside the family or someone who may or may not be in the industry.

Regardless, someday it will happen, and the good news is that you have a choice. That choice is to prepare now so that you will have more control over the situation, which means you'll invariably get more value for your business. Or you can put your head in the sand, continue to be in denial, and wait until that time comes—and then react to the situation. Sort of sounds like going to the dentist, doesn't it? Either you get a checkup on a regular basis or you end up with a rotten tooth and have an ugly situation. Here again, it is "pay me now or pay me later."

Everyone knows that there are "rules of thumb" in every industry. For example, when determining the value of a business, there are rules of thumb about what different businesses are worth. Motels are valued on a multiple times the gross sales, convenience stores are figured on a multiple times the net profit, and service businesses are valued on a multiple of net profit plus equipment. Manufacturing has its rules of thumb, as does the technology business. But did you know that there is a rule of thumb for your foreseeable life expectancy? Yes, as wild as it may sound, there is a rule of thumb to predict how long you will live. Remember, this is just a rule of thumb and not a scientific formula, but it's very interesting.

The rule of thumb for life expectancy is as follows. Subtract your present age from 100, then multiply that number times ⅔, then add that amount back to your present age to get your life expectancy. For example, if you are 55 years old today, then

$$100 - 55 = 45 \times ⅔ = 30 + 55 = 85$$

So, if you are 55 years old today, then you should live to be 85 years old.

OK, I know I don't have any scientific data to confirm this formula, but remember it is a rule of thumb. But what if it is pretty close to being right? There will be an end. Generally, our bodies don't continue at the same rate and energy level we are at today and then suddenly quit working, like batteries in an electronic toy or flashlight. No, we gradually begin to slow down, and the light gets dimmer. Remember, I am not a pessimist, just the opposite. I am a realist.

So, if any of this is true, then why don't we do something about it and get prepared? Even just a little bit prepared . . .

Over the years of helping business owners understand all the ins and outs of selling their business and getting it prepared for sale, I have discovered one thing that helped them get the most value out of the business when it came time to sell. And what was that one thing? Taking the time to prepare themselves and the business in a manner that was practical and understandable to the buyer, regardless of whether the buyer was an outsider or a family member.

I have a lot of respect for business owners who operate their businesses every day. I know how much work it is to keep a business running. There are a million daily distractions when you're trying to grow a business or taking the time to prepare and collect the needed information so that a proper valuation of the business can be done. But generally business owners will put this type of work off, thinking they will get to it later. But later comes faster than we all think. (I, too, ran and operated 40 different businesses, and as they say, "I feel your pain and have walked in your shoes.")

Businesses owners are a unique group of individuals who are generally not given the appreciation and recognition they deserve. They are the ones who make things happen. They are constantly taking action either because they want to or because they must to get something done. Yet, when it comes time to get the most value for them and their families for the equity they have accumulated over many years of hard work, it is sometimes a mystery as to how to get their equity out of the business.

And don't get too excited about the rule of thumb of life expectancy. Who knows? I could be wrong. It could be shorter than we think.

I hope you have been able to extract some information from this book that will give you a realistic view of the enormity involved in the task of selling your business. Years ago, when I owned my businesses, I was not aware that there were people like me who worked and served as professional intermediaries, professionals who could help me understand the process and what was going to be expected of me when it came time to sell my business. Unfortunately, I had to learn the hard way and ended up leaving lots of money on the table because of my ignorance and inexperience.

Now, after being involved in the sale of more than 500 businesses, I am well versed in the process and what will be needed to have a positive outcome when it comes to selling a business. This does not mean I am not still learning, because I am. But what I always share with my clients is that when you work with me, you are acquiring my many years of "expensive experience," thereby hopefully saving you the grief and agony of leaving money on the table the way I have in the past.

Working with professional intermediaries, someone like me and like the American Business Brokers & Advisors, you can rest assured we will always put your interests first. We are realists. All too often people like to look at the world in the way they would like to see it, but that is not always reality. I have learned to deal with what it is and face the reality of the situation.

This doesn't make for the best dinner conversation with my family, but when I'm working with clients, it helps them know they are working in the real world, not in a make-believe, delusional world.

All the best to you. May you continue to enjoy the journey of life we have been so blessed and fortunate to share.

Acknowledgments

I WOULD NOT have been able to start my career in business without the urging of my mother, Violet Monroe, who asked my father, Herschel Monroe, to allow me to work with him in selling oil well interests to investors, which got me started in sales.

Thanks to Pat Niemeyer for giving me the opportunity to begin a career in real estate.

And thanks to Francis Craig for allowing me to be his partner in a venture that later morphed into a chain of 155 video retail stores spanning the United States and Canada.

Thanks to my wife, Sue Monroe, for allowing me the latitude to go forward with the many ventures that I started, invested in, purchased, operated, bought, and sold over the years.

Thanks also to my children—Mandy, Tiffany, and Brittany—for the time I took away from them while I was out on the road wheeling and dealing over the years and not at home being a dad when they were growing up.

Thanks to Bill Fecht for being my partner for more than a decade and introducing me to the many people who helped create the stories in this book.

Thanks to Jon Davito for helping me get started in writing books and teaching me structure and process.

Thanks to Jack Schultz for being gracious with his time and knowledge and resources in helping me perfect my book-writing skills and for his contributions to this book.

And to all the people over the years with whom I have had the opportunity to work in buying, selling, and building businesses. Without them, I would not have been able to acquire the talents and experience (both good and bad) needed to be able to write this book and share my experiences. Thank you.

Index

A

accountants, 104-5, 109-10

American Business Brokers & Advisors (ABBA), 130, 152

Anheuser-Busch, 31-32

attorney, 100-104

B

back-office management staff, 91

Berkshire Hathaway, 146

bookkeeping
  entrepreneurs and, 89-90
  maintaining books, 93-95
  prepping business for sale, 3-4

borrowing
  bank workout department, 44-45
  business expansion and, 27-31
  UCC-1 Financing Statement, 118-19

burnout, as reason for selling business, 20-22

business intermediary, 105-6, 137

"business is my baby" syndrome, 80-81

business owners
  attitude toward selling business, 11-14, 58-59
  commitment to selling process, 111-12
  reasons for selling business, 14-15, 19-50
    burnout, 20-22
    business outgrows the owner, 41-43
    expansion, 27-31
    failing business, 43-46
    fidgeting with business, 33-34
    inability to focus on core business, 46-50
    industry changes, 35-36
    no succession plan, 22-27
    outgrowing the business, 34-35

About the Author

PRESIDENT AND FOUNDER of American Business Brokers & Advisors (ABBA), Terry Monroe, has been in the business of establishing, operating, and selling businesses for more than 30 years. As president of ABBA, which he founded in 1999, he serves as a consultant to business buyers and sellers throughout the nation. His knowledge and expertise in multi-store operations and sales has led to many multimillion-dollar transactions. As an expert source in the convenience store industry, he writes a routine "Financial Insights" guest column for *Convenience Store News* and has been featured in *CSP, CSP Independent, CSNews, Single Store Owner, NPN,* and *National Association of Convenience Stores* magazines.

Terry has been written about and featured in *The Wall Street Journal, Entrepreneur* magazine, CNN Money, and *USA Today*. Over the years, his in-depth knowledge of business enterprising, franchising, financing, and acquisitions has generated over 500 successful transactions.

Terry has been an owner of 40 different businesses, which include 10 national franchises, a franchisor of businesses, and a retailer with more than 200 retail locations within the United States and Canada. The experience of taking his company public, his years of working as a vendor to Wal-Mart Stores, Inc., and of being an owner of restaurants and companies in media and petroleum production and distribution—to name but a few—have given Terry a thorough understanding of business growth and enterprise management, enabling him to provide and share his "expensive experience" with his clients.

A past musician of old rock 'n' roll and an airplane pilot, when not working with his clients, he likes to seek adventure trekking in the mountains. Terry has summited some of the world's most famous peaks, including Mount Kilimanjaro in Africa twice, Mount Aconcagua in Argentina, and Mount Breithorn in Switzerland. His adventurous spirit has taken him river rafting, exploring rainforests in Costa Rica, and on hikes of the Inca Trail to the lost city of Machu Picchu.

Terry has volunteered in fund-raising efforts for the Children's Hospital of Southwest Florida, Hope for Haiti, Naples Community Hospital, and Duke University cancer research.

But the best fun of all is when he gets to spend time with his nine grandchildren.

Terry can be contacted at Terry@TerryMonroe.com.